Mexican Americans

and Language

THE MEXICAN AMERICAN EXPERIENCE

Adela de la Torre, EDITOR

Other books in the series:

Mexican Americans and Language

¡Del dicho al hecho!

Glenn A. Martínez

The University of Arizona Press   Tucson

The University of Arizona Press
© 2006 The Arizona Board of Regents
All rights reserved

⊗ This book is printed on acid-free, archival-quality paper.
Manufactured in the United States of America

11   10   09   08   07   06   6   5   4   3   2   1

Library of Congress Cataloging-in-Publication Data

Martínez, Glenn A., 1971–
Mexican Americans and language : del dicho al hecho /
Glenn A. Martínez.
p. cm. — (The Mexican American experience)
Includes bibliographical references and index.
ISBN-13: 978-0-8165-2374-0 (pbk. : alk. paper)
ISBN-10: 0-8165-2374-6 (pbk. : alk. paper)
1. Linguistic minorities—United States. 2. Mexican Americans—Languages.
3. Second language acquisition. 4. Bilingualism—United States. 5. Code switching
(Linguistics). 6. Spanish language—Variation—United States. 7. English
language—Variation—United States. 8. Ethnicity—United States. 9. National
characteristics—American. I. Title. II. Series.
P119.32.U6M37 2006
306.44089'68073—dc22
2005028392

Publication of this book is made possible in part by the proceeds of a permanent
endowment created with the assistance of a Challenge Grant from the National
Endowment for the Humanities, a federal agency.

■ CONTENTS

ILLUSTRATIONS

FIGURES

TABLES

◼ INTRODUCTION

Outsiders to the Mexican American community may regard language as an incidental characteristic of Mexican American ethnicity. Insiders, however, view it as a defining characteristic. Nowhere have these two attitudes been more evident than in the systematic attack on the use of Spanish in the United States during the late 1980s and into the new millennium. During this period, the "one language" doctrine of Theodore Roosevelt resounded as political activists called for constitutional amendments declaring English the country's official language, rallied for the abolition of bilingual education, and, most recently, fought to strip non-English-speaking citizens of their right to vote. Many Mexican Americans felt that these and other anti-immigrant initiatives were an assault on their cultural heritage and a negation of their rights within an active participatory democracy. More important, these initiatives drove home the increasingly conflictive nature of language in U.S. society.

Every single policy issue that touches the lives of Mexican Americans, be it in the area of health care, fair lending practices, equal access to education, affirmative action, or due process of law, involves language in one way or another. *Mexican Americans and Language* offers a linguistic overview of some of the central issues in the Mexican American **language experience,** giving students the background needed to respond to the multiple social problems that interface with the language differences that exist in the Mexican American minority population.

The language situation of Mexican Americans is extremely complex. This complexity is in large measure a function of the bilingualism of the community that has persisted for more than 150 years. While it is certainly true that large segments of the Mexican American community speak little or no Spanish, it is also true that many do. More often than not, those who speak Spanish and those who don't share a common set of familial, social, and ethnic bonds. This situation makes bilingualism an essential fiber in the lives of all Mexican Americans.

The minority status of Mexican Americans also adds unique dimensions to their language experience. While many perceive bilingualism as an asset, others view it as a barrier to becoming fully American. These **language ideologies** have a powerful influence on the language behavior of the community as a whole. For example, the circulation and imposition of these ideologies in the school system may make children reluctant to speak

Spanish. In the workplace, furthermore, they may disenfranchise workers from management and other leadership positions within their firms. The ideas that have been constructed around the issue of bilingualism both inside and outside the Mexican American community are as important to understanding the Mexican American language experience as bilingualism itself.

This book describes the Mexican American language experience in terms of both bilingualism and minority status. Throughout the text, I will use the term *Mexican American* to refer to Mexican-origin residents of the Southwest, both citizens and noncitizens, who have undergone significant amounts of socialization within the United States. I use the term *Mexican immigrant* to refer to Mexican-origin residents of the Southwest whose socialization occurred largely in Mexico. Chapter 1 deals with language ideologies: We look at the ways in which ideas and beliefs about language arise, how they are circulated, and how they are transgressed on a daily basis by speakers. Chapter 2 deals with language attitudes. We look at the attitudes Mexican American speakers tend to hold about language and how these attitudes fit within the ideological framework that dominates public discourse about Latinas/os in the United States. Chapter 3 deals with **language maintenance** and shift. In this chapter, we look at the mechanisms that induce shift to English versus retention of Spanish in the Mexican American community. Chapter 4 deals with Mexican American Spanish. In this chapter, we focus on the ways that Spanish is used in the Mexican American community. We discuss the processes of language loss that affect speakers' ability to express themselves fluently in Spanish. At the same time, we look at some of the verbal strategies and modalities that distinguish Mexican Americans as a unique language group within the Spanish-speaking world. Chapter 5 deals with Mexican American English and the different sources that are giving rise to a new dialect of American English. We consider the influence of Spanish, African American English, and regional English on the unique ways that Mexican Americans use English. Chapter 6 deals with Mexican American **code switching**; that is, the use of more than one language in a unit of discourse. In this chapter, we consider the motivations that underlie the alternating use of English and Spanish. Each of these chapters ties together the issues of bilingualism and minority status and shows how these strands interface and interact with the Mexican American language experience.

Interspersed within each chapter, you will find topic highlights presenting linguistic facts that can be analyzed using the models and approaches discussed in the chapter. Furthermore, at the end of each chapter is a set of discussion exercises designed to test your command of the concepts illustrated in the chapter. After reading this book I hope you will be able to bridge the gap between *el dicho* (saying) and *el hecho* (doing) and will be able to look at the Mexican American language experience in a way that will encourage you to seek out change and improvement for the Mexican American communities that exist throughout the United States.

Mexican Americans
and Language

Language Ideologies

Bilingualism is beyond a doubt the cornerstone of the Mexican American language experience. The social reality of bilingualism affects all Mexican Americans, whether they speak only English, only Spanish, a little of one language or the other, or a great deal of both. The effects of bilingualism in the daily lives of Mexican Americans range from the routine to the traumatic:

- A schoolgirl's name is changed from San Juanita to Janie because it's easier for the teacher to pronounce.

- A ten-year-old participates in the mother's routine gynecological exam as an interpreter.

- Bullies tease a boy by mimicking his mother's goodbye in broken English.

- A decorated Vietnam veteran is stopped, interrogated, and searched for hours because he "looks and sounds" like a drug dealer.

- A hard-working single mother is accused of child abuse for speaking Spanish to her daughter.

All of these experiences are intimately tied to a social reality of bilingualism, and they are entrenched in the sociocultural presence of two languages (see topic highlight 1).

■ Bilingualism and Language Experience

The importance of bilingualism in the Mexican American language experience has been taken as axiomatic ever since the language varieties of Mexican Americans first began attracting scholarly attention nearly one hundred years ago.[1] The way that bilingualism has been defined, however, has indelibly marked both the direction of research and the subsequent findings and interpretations. Bilingualism has been defined from at least three different perspectives: the linguistic perspective, the sociolinguistic perspective, and the critical perspective.

Topic Highlight 1. **The Experience of Bilingualism**

José Antonio Burciaga vividly recounts the experience of bilingualism in his recollection of growing up in El Paso, Texas. Burciaga reflects on the day his parents took the oath to become U.S. citizens. He writes, "And so, despite their limited English, my parents became U.S. citizens. They knew what *weedee peepo* meant. It meant *Nosotros el pueblo,* We the people. Whatever language we speak, we have the same goals stated in our Constitution" (Burciaga 1988, 58).

Burciaga argues that his parents became U.S. citizens and participated in the American dream and the American promise "despite their limited English." While Burciaga focuses on the absence of English, I would prefer to underscore the presence of Spanish. Burciaga's parents claimed their place in U.S. society as *weedee peepo, nosotros el pueblo, en inglés y en español.* This is a powerful reminder of the central role of bilingualism—the presence of both Spanish and English—in Mexican American lives and communities. ■

The Linguistic Perspective

The linguistic perspective on bilingualism focuses on the language system itself. The noted American linguist Leonard Bloomfield defined bilingualism as "a native-like control of two or more languages" (Bloomfield 1933, 56). The key word in Bloomfield's definition is *control.* For Bloomfield, bilingualism is a cognitive reality that exists in the mind of an individual speaker. Thus, to study bilingualism is to study the individual mind and how it deals with and controls two different languages. This approach to bilingualism has been prevalent in the study of Mexican American language. Scholars working within these parameters have tirelessly endeavored to dissect the linguistic system of Mexican American speakers into its component parts: **phonology, morphology, syntax, semantics,** and the **lexicon.** Then, they have proceeded to compare each part with other varieties of Spanish or English in order to describe how Mexican American speech "deviates" from other ways of speaking. The major impetus in these studies, then, has been to describe the nature and characteristics of the two languages that Mexican American speakers possess and compare them with other languages spoken outside of the Mexican American community.

The Sociolinguistic Perspective

The sociolinguistic approach to bilingualism focuses less on the linguistic system itself than on how that system is deployed in different social encounters. Uriel Weinreich, whose foundational work *Languages in Contact* is still widely consulted in the field of bilingualism, defined "the practice of alternatively using two languages . . . [as] bilingualism, and the persons involved bilinguals" (Weinreich 1953, 5). Notice that the key word in Weinreich's definition is not *controlling* two language systems, as it is in Bloomfield's definition, but rather *using* two languages. For Weinreich, then, bilingualism is a social reality that exists in the routine encounters of different individuals involved in different social practices. While the use of two languages implies that the speaker has a reasonable degree of control over each of them, it also extends beyond the issue of control to include issues such as the social reasons for using different languages at different times, in different places, and with different people. Thus, to study bilingualism is to study how speakers use different languages in different social situations. Charles Ferguson summed up this approach well in his now-famous question: Who speaks what language to whom, when?

The sociolinguistic approach to Mexican American language has also become firmly established over the years. In this vein, scholars have attempted to decipher how Mexican American speakers determine when to speak English, when to speak Spanish, and when to use a little of both. They thus have tried to discover patterns of language behaviors in bilingual Mexican American communities and to shed light on the **functional domains**—people, places, or topics where a language is favored—that correspond with the distinctive language behaviors present in the community. They also have examined how the distribution of languages across functional domains interacts with the ultimate survival or demise of each language in contact. For instance, if one language is used in functional domains that are infrequent, such as family gatherings, interactions with grandparents, and the like, and the other in functional domains that are relatively frequent, such as at work, at school, and with members of the immediate family, then we might surmise that the language used less frequently is likely to disappear within a few generations. Similarly, these studies have shed light on the formal properties of the languages in question. For instance, we would expect that when a person seldom uses a language, his or her comfort level with the grammar and the vocabulary of that language would diminish. Sociolinguistic studies of the Mexican American community have shown that many speakers feel "rusty" in their Spanish and these feelings do in fact show up in the ways they use the language. The sociolinguistic perspective on bilingualism differs fundamentally from the linguistic perspective because it goes beyond the study of language systems and examines how those systems function in social settings.

The Critical Linguistic Perspective

Like the linguistic and sociolinguistic approaches, critical linguistic perspectives on bilingualism try to explain both the formal manifestations of languages in contact and the functional distribution of these languages. Critical approaches to bilingualism differ, however, in that they focus on the uses of the two languages as a reflection of the ideological systems of dominance and subordination that underpin social hierarchies. In other words, this view of bilingualism takes into account not only the linguistic and social manifestations of language contact, but the political ramifications as well. Catherine Walsh defines critical bilingualism as "the ability to not just speak two languages, but to be conscious of the sociocultural, political, and ideological contexts in which the languages (and therefore the speakers) are positioned and function, and of the multiple meanings that are fostered in each" (Walsh 1991, 126–27). So, rather than looking at formal features of Mexican American Spanish or English as deviations from some norm or as cases of bilingual interference, critical linguists focus instead on how these formal features are used in order to subvert Mexican American speakers and to keep them out of privileged positions. Similarly, instead of focusing on when and where speakers choose to speak a particular language, they prefer to ask why a given language is reserved for a particular function, and what social and political significance emerges from that distribution of use. Ana Celia Zentella sums up the critical perspective on bilingualism as an approach that attempts "to understand and facilitate a stigmatized group's attempts to construct a positive self within an economic and political context that relegates its members to static and disparaged ethnic, racial, and class identities, and that identifies them with static and disparaged linguistic codes" (Zentella 1997, 13). So, the critical view of bilingualism differs fundamentally from linguistic and sociolinguistic approaches in that it goes beyond description and explanation and calls for action in realizing certain political goals as well.

While the critical view of bilingualism has just recently begun to attract the attention of linguists in professional circles, it has been a fundamental driving force behind much of the research carried out in the context of the Mexican American community over the past century, as I hope to demonstrate. At this point, however, it seems important to underscore that the critical approach to bilingualism does not disparage or dispense with linguistic or sociolinguistic approaches to the linguistic realities of Mexican American speakers. What it does is to take this knowledge, both linguistic and sociolinguistic, and contextualize and problematize it within a specific political agenda that will lead to important political gains within the community under investigation. It attempts to bridge the gap between *el dicho* (saying) and *el hecho* (doing); a challenging task indeed, for as the saying goes, *del dicho al hecho hay mucho trecho* (from word to deed is a long way indeed).

These varying approaches to bilingualism—linguistic, sociolinguistic, and critical linguistic—underscore the richness of the study of **language experience.** A language experience is more than just the language itself and more than the deployment of the language in social situations. A language experience is the composite of a group's experience with, in, and through language. In order to study language experience, then, we must look at the complex intersections between multiple facets of language including language structure, language use, language politics, language history, language attitudes, **language ideologies,** and so on. As we focus our attention on the language experience of Mexican Americans, therefore, we will attend to each of these facets in different ways. For instance, we will survey language structure and use as we look at the features and processes that characterize Mexican American Spanish, Mexican American English, and Mexican American **code switching.** Similarly, we will survey language history as we examine the historic and ongoing tensions between **language maintenance** and **language shift.** We will see how particular historical events and their interactions with existing or emerging social institutions serve at times to buffer the language shift process and at other times to weaken community support for language maintenance. We will survey language attitudes in the Mexican American community as we review some of the social psychological, anthropological, and sociolinguistic studies of Mexican American perceptions and beliefs about language. We will also look at some of the ways in which Mexican American language has been viewed by the dominant culture, and how these perceptions and beliefs interact with the perceptions and beliefs of the subordinate culture. As we study language ideologies, we will come across a series of fundamental tensions in the social and political arena. Such tensions seem to me to be the central and defining components of the Mexican American language experience, and thus, I will begin there.

■ Features of Language Ideologies

It may seem odd that words like *language* and *ideology* should appear together in the same phrase. We would not normally associate something like language, perceived as neutral and not inherently in the interest of any particular person or group, with something like ideology, perceived as politically charged and specifically geared toward the advancement of a particular interest or agenda. People generally think of language as something that allows us to communicate with others, that brings us closer through dialogue.

While this is certainly one function of language, language also divides us through difference. You may very well understand what I am saying but be absolutely turned off by the way I say it. Linguists and sociologists of language have long recognized this dual aspect of language. The ways we use language often indicate, or index, the group or groups we identify with, and thus fit like hand in glove into the social hierarchies that characterize our collective existence. What this means is that, as social beings, we tend to associate certain values and beliefs with different groups of people, and the language that is characteristic of these groups then serves as an index of those values and beliefs. In this way, then, we can talk specifically about language ideologies and define them, following Michael Silverstein, as "a set of beliefs about language articulated by users as a rationalization or justification of perceived language structure and use" (Silverstein 1979, 193).

Language ideology is couched in language variation. To be a speaker of a language is to be able to adopt a particular shared pattern of verbal behavior. However, the degree to which that behavior conforms to or diverges from the shared pattern varies from person to person and from group to group. The degree to which our speech patterns conform to or differ from one another has to do with our lived experiences in social encounters. Language ideologies are thus embodied in these lived experiences. Louis-Jean Calvet, in fact, characterizes these oppositional lived experiences as the basis for "language wars." He writes, "if humanity, then, entered into linguistic communication through multilingualism, it has at the same time dealt with multilingualism through condemning others. By converting differences into subordination, by considering the language of others as inferior, even as non-language, right from the beginning human beings have laid down the premises of a war of languages" (Calvet 1998, 51). Just as military conflicts socially manage and politically control territories and the people who inhabit them, so language wars, through language ideologies, socially manage and politically control language differences and the people who use those differences in routine speech events. Language ideologies are, then, fundamentally about social and political control of linguistically distinct groups. With an understanding of language ideologies as "regimes of language," we can now proceed to describe at least four facets of language ideologies as they relate to the language experiences of Mexican Americans.[2]

Ideology as Interest

First, *a language ideology represents a perception of language and discourse that is constructed in the interest of a specific social or cultural group*. This suggests that every language group constructs a set of beliefs about language in order to serve its own interests. The word *ideology* itself, coined by Napoleon, emerged as a derogatory word referring to the false beliefs of powerful groups (Braybrooke 1967, 124–27). Now, however, we understand an ideology not only as something possessed by the powerful, but also as something that is used and possessed by the powerless in order to challenge the perpetuation of asymmetric power relations (Eagleton 1991, 6–7). No language group is, therefore, non-ideological. A language group may consider itself neutral; however, this neutrality is itself ideological. Consider, for instance, what is often referred to as "network American English." This particular variety of American English, characteristic of the Midwest and the standard for broadcast journalism, is often heralded as just "plain old" English, a variety of English that does not betray allegiance to any particular history or ethnicity. But the very fact that a particular variety is perceived as "colorless," "characterless," or "boring" in and of itself bespeaks of a language ideology, a set of beliefs that justifies language use. So in essence every language group builds up language ideologies that support and sustain its own linguistic and sociolinguistic practices.

Topic Highlight 2. Language Panic in Arizona's Proposition 203

Arizona's Proposition 203, which called for the abolition of bilingual education in Arizona public schools, constituted a language panic. Consider the language used in the Findings and Declarations of the proposition.

1. The English language is the national public language of the United States of America and of the state of Arizona. It is spoken by the vast majority of Arizona residents, and is also the leading world language for science, technology, and international business, thereby being the language of economic opportunity; and

2. Immigrant parents are eager to have their children acquire a good knowledge of English, thereby allowing them to fully participate in the American Dream of economic and social advancement; and

3. The government and the public schools of Arizona have a moral obligation and a constitutional duty to provide all of Arizona's children, regardless of their ethnicity or national origins, with the skills necessary to become productive members of our society. Of these skills, literacy in the English language is among the most important.

4. The public schools of Arizona currently do an inadequate job of educating immigrant children, wasting financial resources on costly experimental language programs whose failure over the past two decades is demonstrated by the current high drop-out rates and low English literacy levels of many immigrant children.

5. Young immigrant children can easily acquire full fluency in a new language, such as English, if they are heavily exposed to that language in the classroom at an early age.

6. Therefore it is resolved that: all children in Arizona public schools shall be taught English as rapidly and effectively as possible.

7. Under circumstances in which portions of this statute are subject to conflicting interpretations, these Findings and Declarations shall be assumed to contain the governing intent of the statute (Available online at *James Crawford's Language Policy Web Site and Emporium*. Available at: http://ourworld.compuserve.com/homepages/JWCRAWFORD/echar.htm. Downloaded 6 February 2004).

Now consider the following questions:

- How does the language of the proposition create an elevated place for English and a subservient one for Spanish?
- What constitutive metaphors about English appear in the text?
- How did the writers of the proposition disparage the Spanish language without ever mentioning it? ■

With respect to the Mexican American language experience, this generalization has important implications. First, we realize that just as Mexican Americans construct ideologies about their own language behavior and that of dominant groups, so dominant groups also construct ideologies about Mexican American language behavior. In other words, language ideologies are oppositional in the sense that one always challenges and attempts to subvert the other. We could take this a step further and try to identify the language ideologies that prevail in dominant groups.

Jane Hill proposes that one manifestation of a dominant language ideology can be found in what she calls "language panics." A language panic is a period of intense debate and heightened emotions over relatively obscure and technical issues. Questions such as, "Should we understand African American English to be a dialect of English or, because of its African substratum, to be a distinct language?" and "Precisely what mix of mother tongue and target language in the primary school classroom makes for the most effective student achievement?" are examples of language panic (Hill 2001, 249). Such questions erupt into heated debates at certain historical junctures, such as the debates over Proposition 227 in California and Proposition 203 in Arizona (both anti–bilingual education initiatives) or the controversy when the Oakland School District proposed to provide academic instruction in Ebonics (African American English), both of which sparked massive national and international attention in the late 1990s. Hill asks why such technical matters should stir up so much animosity within our society. Her answer is that because underneath these technical issues lie fundamental issues about racial relations in our society (see topic highlight 2).

But I understand language panics in a broader and more continuous

Topic Highlight 3. **Mock Spanish in the Southwest**

"Mock Spanish" has been used extensively in the Southwest for numerous purposes. Consider the following joke from a 1943 collection of Texas jests:

> A newcomer in the border country heard nothing except *mañana* and *¿Quién sabe?* (literally, "Who knows?" but, accompanied by a shrug of the shoulders, a lift of the eyebrow, a roll of the eyes and a quick movement of the hands, it can mean everything or nothing).
>
> One day he saw a funeral procession and, noticing a particularly intelligent-looking Mexican who—he figured—could speak English, the newcomer inquired:
>
> "Who's dead?"
>
> There came the inevitable "*¿Quién sabe?*"
>
> "Fine," said the Easterner, "and I hope that other so-and-so, *mañana,* dies right away too." (House 1943, 77)

What are the functions of mock Spanish in the joke? ■

sense than a heightened emotional concern about technical linguistic issues at particular historical junctures. Language panic is also manifested in more routine affairs such as what Hill calls "mock Spanish"—that is, the overly anglicized use of Spanish that corresponds with violence, *Hasta la vista, Baby*, with hypersexuality, *caliente mamacita*, with subservience, *sí, Señor*, or with laziness, *mañana* (see topic highlight 3).

Similarly, language panic shows up in other routine behaviors such as what Zentella identifies as "dialect dissing"—the elevation of standard and European dialects of Spanish over Mexican American dialects of Spanish—and "Spanglish bashing"—the pejorative view of code switching as "a deficient code spoken by deficient speakers and responsible for their academic failure" (Zentella 2002, 328). I would argue, then, together with Hill that all of these manifestations of language panic—ranging from the routine to the extraordinary—serve as instances in which "whiteness" and its signatory, indexical language, plain English, are elevated. At the same time, they represent racialized others as a problem.

POCHO.COM™
SPANGLISH IS MY LANGUAGE
SATIRE, NEWS Y CHAT
FOR THE SPANGLISH
GENERATION

■ 1. The masthead of Pocho.com magazine illustrates semantic inversion in its adoption of the slogan "Spanglish is my language." (Courtesy of Pocho.com magazine)

On the other hand, we can also identify an oppositional ideology that challenges language panics; namely, language pride. I understand language pride as the belief that the language of one's home and community is a viable public language and a real option to be used and infused in expressing one's voice. In the Mexican American community, language pride surfaces in multiple ways. Flores and Yúdice describe linguistic "inventiveness" as one manifestation of language pride:

> Language itself, of course, is the most obvious site of Latino inventiveness. Whether the wildest extravagance of the bilingual poet or the most mundane comment of everyday life, Latino usage tends necessarily toward interlingual innovation. The interfacing of multiple codes serves to decanonize all of them, at least in their presumed discrete authority, thus allowing ample space for spontaneous experimentation and punning. Even for the most monolingual of Latinos, the "other" language looms constantly as a potential resource, and the option to vary according to speech contexts is used far more often than not. (Flores and Yúdice 1997, 190–91)

Zentella, along similar lines, identifies pride in the transformation and inversion of derogatory labels. She argues that "more and more young Latina/os are reflecting this positive stance by transforming labels like 'Spanglish,' 'Nuyorican,' 'Chicano,' and 'Dominican York' through the process of **semantic** inversion and adopting them with pride" (Zentella 2003, 57). Mexican American political satirist Lalo Alacaraz, for example, adopts the slogan "Spanglish is my language" for his online magazine *Pocho.com* (see figure 1). In this way, both language panic and language pride highlight the interests that underlie language ideologies.

Multiplicity of Ideologies

A second point to be made about language ideologies is that *ideologies are profitably conceived of as multiple because of the multiplicity of meaningful social divisions within sociocultural groups that have the potential to produce divergent perspectives expressed as indices of group membership.* On the one hand, multiplicity can be viewed as binary and oppositional in the tensions between language pride and language panic. Following Norma González, however, the perspective of language ideologies actually allows us to "fracture the 'one language—one culture' isomorphism of Spanish speaking populations as we become aware of, for instance, the derogation of Chicano Spanish by native Spanish speakers" (González 2001, 178). What this means is that multiple language ideologies may exist within a single racial or ethnic group. In other words, it would be a grave error to suppose that language pride is always and only expressed and reproduced within the Mexican American community and that language panic is always and only expressed and reproduced within the dominant culture. In fact, what we find from inside both communities is precisely the opposite. As González points out, the routine activities of "dialect dissing" and "Spanglish bashing" are just as common inside the Mexican American community as they are outside it. But instances of language panic are sometimes more subtle than any direct disparagement of verbal behavior. Otto Santa Ana, for example, argues that much of the ideological content of language panics is contained in subtle but deeply entrenched metaphors. So, even within the Mexican American community we can find the racializing functions of language panics. One example might be the metaphor that views English as just natural. This metaphor substantiates many of the basic claims against bilingual education. "For Americans," writes Santa Ana, "the English language is not really a language—it's just English—namely, that way of talking that is naturally a complete, lucid and fully sufficient medium for all social intercourse in America" (Santa Ana 2002, 211). The fluid nature of English is also apparent in much of the marketing of English skills within the Mexican American community. The fluidity of English is embodied in its ability to carry things, more specifically, to carry people down the stream toward material prosperity:

> In Spanish language television programming, advertising for *Inglés sin barreras,* a pricey English-language instruction program, promises success and riches as a consequence of learning English. English is a "jewel that no one can take away from you" and the "passport that no one can rescind," claim the ads. Children are sometimes portrayed overhearing their parents' struggles with lack of employment opportunities and advancement

because they don't understand English, and the commercials claim that "every day that goes by without speaking English is money that is lost." (González 2001, 178)

But language panic need not even be expressed in the interest of English hegemony. Frances Aparicio, for instance, notes that many anglicized Latinas/os feel the brunt of not speaking Spanish or not speaking it "well" through epithets such as "el hijo de Pete Wilson" (son of [conservative former California governor] Pete Wilson; Aparicio 2000, 269). The multiplicity of language ideologies within the Mexican American community suggests that there is no one Mexican American language ideology, but rather that a confluence of ideologies emerges from within and from without, penetrating inwards and extending outwards.

Flexible Nature of Ideology

A third point about language ideologies is that *group members may display varying degrees of awareness of local language ideologies*. The degree of awareness a speaker has is not necessarily correlated with his or her competence or actual use of a given language. Specifically, it is not the case that all and only monolingual English-speaking Mexican Americans express and reproduce language panic nor that all and only bilingual Mexican Americans express and reproduce language pride. There is in fact little correlation between language proficiency and pride versus panic. This fact has led Ana Celia Zentella, for instance, to remark that "U.S. Latinos of all generations are redefining their native cultures without a language requirement" (Zentella 2002, 332). Frances Aparicio, furthermore, probed the language ideologies of English-speaking Latina/o college students at a major university in the Midwest. With regard to English-speaking Mexican Americans she concluded:

> Negotiating between their American-ness—their "being" in and through the English language—and their *latinidad,* socially mediated through Spanish, Anglophone Latina/os redefine the role of language in the construction of their own, hybrid cultural identity . . . the linguistic knowledge and grammatical mastery that educators use as a basis for defining competency are not necessarily the criteria used by these students to define their connection to Spanish. They defined their possession of the language more in terms of symbolic and affective capital. (Aparicio 2000, 271)

So, even if they could not speak the language, these students still evinced a robust language pride in Spanish that challenged and subverted language panic in important and profound ways.

Ideology as Mediated

A final point to be made with respect to language ideologies is that *members' language ideologies mediate between social structures and forms of talk.* This means that speakers bridge linguistic difference and sociocultural experience through the construction of ideologies. In other words, language pride and language panic, as explicitly identifiable ideologies in the Mexican American community, serve to connect the language they speak and hear with their everyday experience as members of a minority group. Irvine and Gal identify three processes that can be thought of as the building blocks of ideologies.

Iconization "involves a transformation of the sign relationship between linguistic features and the social images with which they are linked" (Irvine and Gal 2000, 37). This process is widely observed in the construction of language ideologies among Mexican Americans. For example, code switching is widely disparaged as an "inferior" language form; yet many young Mexican Americans have transformed the social image of code switching to signify a positive feature of ethnic identity. Carmen Fought, in her study of Chicano English in southern California, found that many youngsters iconized code switching as an essential part of Mexican American identity. "Sí, hablan chicano, Chicano language" (Yes, they speak Chicano), reports her informant (Fought 2003, 209). Conversely, language behavior has also been iconized in favor of language panic. Aparicio, for example, notes that the "European American–dominant society represses Spanish by evoking images of poverty and economic marginality" (Aparicio 2000, 258).

A second process identified by Irvine and Gal is *fractal recursivity,* which "involves the projection of an opposition, salient at some level of relationship, onto some other level" (Irvine and Gal 2000, 38). What this means is that some opposition, for example the opposition between Spanish and English, is displaced from one level of relationship—a defining national symbol—and reconstituted at another level—the act of participating in a social activity or ritual. Zentella identifies fractal recursivity with precision when she argues that "Spanglish, the **alternation** of several dialects of Spanish and English so challenges the notion of bounded languages and identities that any effort to halt the crossing of linguistic boundaries seems as foolhardy as the proverbial finger in the dike" (Zentella 2003, 61). Notice here that the process of fractal recursivity allows individuals to redefine and reconstitute the basic assumptions of oppositional language ideologies.

The final process identified by Irvine and Gal is *erasure*. This is "the process in which ideology, in simplifying the sociolinguistic field, renders some persons or activities invisible" (Irvine and Gal 2000, 38). This process can be seen quite clearly in the case of Anglophone Mexican Americans who struggle with an ethnic "invisibility" imposed upon them by the ideology that equates Mexicanness with knowing Spanish. One of Fought's respondents gives a candid view of erasure:

> "When people ask me [about my ethnicity]," she remarks, "I say Mexican but, but then they say, 'No you're not. You don't speak Spanish.' They, they just tease me to get me mad. . . . I guess a lot of people think if you don't speak Spanish you're not like full Mexican or whatever, but, but I am! I—I think so." (Fought 2003, 201)

The processes of iconicity, fractal recursivity, and erasure thus constitute some of the ways in which speakers connect language with their lived experience as persons of minority status.

Concluding Thoughts

As we have seen in this chapter, the Mexican American language experience cannot be studied apart from bilingualism. At the same time, however, bilingualism can be approached from at least three distinct perspectives. The linguistic approach focuses on the interactions between coexisting language systems in an individual's mind and that speaker's command of the two languages. The sociolinguistic approach focuses on the interactions between coexisting language groups living in a single social order. The critical approach looks at the nature of the social interactions engendered by a bilingual reality and attempts to configure these interactions within the larger ideological constructs that sustain privilege and power in the prevailing social order. To study bilingualism from this perspective, then, it is important to delineate what language ideologies are and how they take shape within the context of the Mexican American experience.

I identified two opposing language ideologies in the Mexican American language experience—language pride and language panic—and showed how these ideologies are constructed and reproduced in both the bilingual

Mexican American community and the monolingual dominant culture. Finally, I argued that there is a fundamental tension between the ideologies of language pride and language panic, a tension that permeates the entire Mexican American language experience. As we continue our survey, we will pay close attention to how these two ideologies manifest themselves in different facets of the language experience.

■ Discussion Exercises

1. Compare and contrast the three approaches to the study of bilingualism discussed in this chapter.

2. Describe the concept of a language experience. Try to characterize your own language experience in a short paragraph.

3. Why do speakers tend to form ideologies about language? What social functions do language ideologies serve?

4. Identify and describe three constitutive elements of language panics.

5. How does language pride interrupt language panic?

6. What role does English play in language pride and in language panic? How do monolingual English-speaking Mexican Americans use English in constructing language pride?

7. Identify and discuss the processes that mediate language use and social structure. Describe how these processes are deployed in the context of the Mexican American language experience.

8. The process of erasure consists of a simplification of the sociolinguistic field that renders certain persons or activities invisible. Describe how this process has been enacted in your own language experience.

■ Suggested Readings

González, Norma. *I Am My Language: Discourses of Women and Children in the Borderlands*. Tucson: University of Arizona Press, 2001.

Kroskrity, Paul V., ed. *Regimes of Language: Ideologies, Polities, and Identities*. Santa Fe, NM: School of American Research Press, 2000.

Lippi-Green, Rosina. *English with an Accent: Language, Ideology, and Discrimination in the United States*. New York: Routledge, 1997.

Santa Ana, Otto. *Brown Tide Rising: Metaphors of Latinos in Contemporary American Public Discourse*. Austin: University of Texas Press, 2002.

Urciuoli, Bonnie. *Exposing Prejudice: Puerto Rican Experiences of Language, Race, and Class*. Boulder, CO: Westview Press, 1996.

■ Notes

1. The first linguistic study of Mexican American language was conducted in the late nineteenth century as a doctoral dissertation project by the noted New Mexican scholar Aurelio M. Espinosa.

2. I follow Kroskrity (2000) in making these points.

Language Attitudes

In the previous chapter we discussed a **language ideology** as a system of beliefs that work together to the benefit or detriment of particular social groups. In this chapter we will explore the relationship between language attitudes and language ideologies: how individual attitudes about language fit into the wider ideological systems that define the Mexican American **language experience.** In attempting to answer this question, we will consider attitudes about language and identity, language variation, and **language maintenance,** and finally, we will see how these attitudes feed into the oppositional ideologies of language pride and language panic.

Attitudes and Ideologies

An attitude can be defined as a "response that locates objects of thought on dimensions of judgment" (McGuire 1985, 239). When we talk about language attitudes, then, we are referring to the ways individuals locate language-related concepts—for instance, languages themselves, bilingualism, language varieties, and so on—on different dimensions of judgment such as good or bad, beautiful or ugly, useful or useless. In a sense, when we discussed language ideologies in the previous chapter, we were talking about language attitudes. There are however some important differences between the concept of language ideology and the concept of language attitude.

First of all, a language ideology serves a particular function in the language community where it flourishes. The same is not always true of a language attitude. Humberto López Morales argues that attitudes serve a multiplicity of purposes in the lives of speakers and their languages (López Morales 1993, 236). A language attitude can only be considered ideological when it serves to "promote and legitimize" the power status of a particular group (Eagleton 1991, 29). If it does not serve the interests of one group vis-à-vis another, then the attitude is probably not ideological. So, while all language ideologies include language attitudes, not all language attitudes constitute ideologies.

This brings us to the second difference between language attitudes and language ideologies. Language ideologies involve "multiple objects of thought projected on multiple dimensions of judgment" (McGuire 1985, 248). In other words, a language ideology is a structured constellation of attitudes about different aspects of language that justifies and rationalizes particular power relations in a society. Language attitudes, then, can be considered the building blocks of a language ideology. Ideologies are constructed from attitudes and are then used to achieve certain sociopolitical goals.

A language attitude consists of affective, behavioral, and cognitive dimensions. For example, suppose that John has a negative attitude toward Southern American English. In the cognitive dimension, he may have certain ideas about Southern American English that reflect his negative attitude. He might believe that southerners sound lazy and unprofessional, that they do not make a concerted effort to speak properly, and so on. In the affective dimension, southern speech may elicit certain negative emotions and feelings. Perhaps these negative feelings are connected with someone John knows who speaks that way. In the behavioral dimension, he may avoid associating with people who speak that way (Baker 1992, 12–13). So, an attitude is really a combination of ideas and beliefs, feelings and emotions, and actions and reactions.

An attitude is normally individual. An ideology, on the other hand, is aggregative, or collective. This is true in two different ways. An attitude is individual in the sense that normally one response is associated with one object of thought, and it is also individual in that the response is characteristic of an individual person. An ideology is aggregative in the sense that it normally involves multiple and systematic responses to multiple and systematic objects of thought. It is also aggregative in the sense that it is shared by a group of individuals in order to promote and legitimize the group as a whole. In sum, we can think of the relationship between attitudes and ideologies as a hierarchy where a combination of ideas and beliefs, feelings and emotions, and actions and reactions make up an attitude and where a combination of attitudes make up an ideology. The relationship between language attitudes and language ideologies makes language attitude studies an important site for the investigation of language ideologies.

The connection between attitude and action merits further discussion. An attitude can be described as a predisposition toward a given reaction in a given situation. So, for instance, Frederick Williams defined *attitude* as "an internal state aroused by stimulation of some type and which may mediate the organism's subsequent response" (Fasold 1987, 147). We might expect, therefore, that if Mary holds a negative attitude toward a particular speech pattern, she would be predisposed to react in a negative manner when confronted with that speech pattern. We might further speculate that she would resist adopting such a speech pattern unless some person or event were to drastically change her attitude.

While this assumption seems logical, in practice we find an altogether different state of affairs. For instance, most language groups of the world construct certain norms, or standards, that identify certain words or phrases as incorrect, bad usage, or slang. In English class, we are often taught, and therefore believe, that using words such as *ain't* or ending a sentence in a preposition constitutes "bad usage." Despite this conditioning, however, many of us continue to say *ain't* and to end sentences in prepositions. Why do we persist in a given behavior even when our attitude toward it is negative? Sociolinguists have for quite some time noted that speakers of the vernacular (that is, a nonstandard dialect), even while using it in real communicative events, often hold extremely negative attitudes toward it, characterizing it as "bad" or "broken" language. In order to deal with these apparent contradictions, sociolinguists have proposed a distinction between **overt prestige** and **covert prestige.** Overt prestige is when a speaker explicitly identifies positive attitudes toward a particular language behavior. Covert prestige is when a speaker implicitly identifies positive attitudes toward a particular language behavior—not by identifying the behavior as positive or good, but rather by performing it in real communicative settings (Holmes 1992, 344–57).

This distinction emerges because language attitudes are essentially multifunctional. On the one hand, a language attitude serves an integrative function when a speaker's positive attitude toward a given behavior serves to unite that speaker with a particular group. On the other hand, a language attitude serves an instrumental function when a speaker's positive attitude toward a given behavior results in some personal material or symbolic gain for that speaker. We might wonder whether integration is not in and of itself also instrumental, inasmuch as it represents a personal material and symbolic gain for the speaker. In many cases this may be true, but usually gain occurs when the group one wants to be associated with holds power in a given society. When the group one belongs to is not in a position of power, however, we begin to understand the motivations behind covert prestige. A person may want to obtain the benefits associated with being part of one group and on those grounds hold positive attitudes toward the language of that group. At the same time, this person may also want to identify himself or herself with a different group and on those grounds hold positive attitudes toward this second group even if these attitudes are counter to the values and beliefs of the first group.

The functions of language attitudes, moreover, play out in different fields. It is one thing to identify intrinsically, or covertly, with a linguistic group by using words and phrases normally associated with that group. It is quite another thing to extrinsically identify with that group by openly and adamantly defending their ways of speaking. In other words, there are two functions of language attitudes—instrumental and integrative—and also two orientations in which actions based on language attitudes unfold—intrinsic and extrinsic. So, when looking at attitudes we can visualize them as being graphed along two perpendicular axes, where the x axis represents the functions of attitudes (ranging from integrative to instrumental) and the y axis represents the orientations of attitudes (ranging from intrinsic to extrinsic). When we look at attitudes in this way, we can see that four possible dimensions emerge corresponding to the four quadrants: intrinsic instrumental attitudes, extrinsic instrumental attitudes, intrinsic integrative attitudes, and extrinsic integrative attitudes. These dimensions define what function an attitude accomplishes and the particular orientation in which it is being accomplished. Hofman sums this up as follows:

> An intrinsic view takes the form of sentimentalism when it has to do with private enjoyment of language; it becomes a value when the language appears to represent interpersonal or public symbols. An extrinsic view becomes instrumentalism in the private mode and communication in the public one, depending on whether a language is considered in terms of private or public advantages respectively. (quoted in Mejías, Anderson-Mejías, and Carlson 2003, 142)

On the basis of the intersection between function and orientation, therefore, Hofman recognizes four dimensions of language attitudes: sentimental, value or loyalty, instrumentalism, and communication (see figure 2).

Extrinsic

open support for
language code

Communication

Instrumental
material rewards

Language
Attitudes

Loyalty

Integrative
group belonging

Instrumentalism

Sentimentalism

Intrinsic

use but not open
support for
language code

■ 2. Four dimensions of language attitudes.

Language attitudes in the Mexican American community often display tensions between overt and covert prestige, between instrumental and integrative functions, and between extrinsic and intrinsic orientations. I mentioned earlier that the ideological context in which Mexican American language experiences are lived out is characterized by a fundamental tension between language pride and language panic. This ideological tension emerges from the tensions between the constitutive attitudes that make up the ideologies of language pride and language panic. In order to uncover this tension more fully, let's look at language attitudes from three different perspectives and try to identify how these attitudes reflect both language pride and language panic.

The first perspective has to do with the relationship speakers perceive between language and identity. In other words, how strongly do Mexican Americans feel that the presence of Spanish is a defining characteristic of their ethnic identity in the United States? The second perspective relates to attitudes toward language variation in the Mexican American community: What types of Spanish do Mexican Americans perceive within their communities, and how do they react to these different varieties? How do Mexican Americans perceive the practice of **code switching?** What values do they assign to this linguistic behavior? The third perspective has to do with attitudes toward language maintenance: Is it important to keep the Spanish language alive in the Mexican American community? Whose responsibility is it to make sure that Spanish survives in the long term? As we examine these perspectives, we should keep in mind how each perspective fits into a larger ideological formation that serves to promote and legitimize a unique place for Mexican Americans in American life and, at the same time, to challenge and subvert those ideologies that would attempt to erase the Mexican from Mexican American.

■ Attitudes about Language and Identity

Many attitude studies in Mexican American communities have set out to determine the relative importance of speaking Spanish in the construction of a Mexican American ethnic identity. These studies have been carried out using **sociolinguistic questionnaires** that ask direct or indirect questions about the relationship between language and identity. The questions are posed to a cross section of the population under investigation and the results are statistically tallied in order to uncover generalizations about the nature and distribution of a particular attitude. The most common question asked in this type of study is, *Is Spanish an important part of being Hispanic/Latino(a)/Mexican American?* Some studies find huge disparities in attitudes between age groups and levels of assimilation, and other studies find fairly uniform attitudes across the board.

Looking at this attitude in terms of the four-way division sketched out in figure 2, we might say that attitudes about the role of language as a marker of group identity are *extrinsically* oriented and serve an *integrative* function. In other words, attitudes about language and identity are located in the *loyalty* quadrant of the chart. So, in the next few paragraphs we will try to get a sense of the overall Spanish language loyalty of the Mexican American community.

Susana Rivera-Mills carried out a sociolinguistic study of language attitudes in the northern California community of Fortuna. In her study, she looked at the language attitudes of a mixed Spanish-speaking community consisting of Mexicans, U.S.–born Latinos, Salvadorans, and other Latino groups. She surveyed a total of fifty respondents equally divided by gender, nationality, and social class. She also considered recency of immigration as an important variable. Three generational groups of immigrants are commonly defined in the literature: First-generation immigrants are those who were born outside of the United States and typically arrived in this country as older children or adults; second-generation immigrants are those who were born in the United States of foreign-born parents; and third-generation immigrants are those who were born in the United States but whose grandparents were foreign-born.

In her questionnaire Rivera-Mills included the statement: *To be Hispanic you must speak Spanish.* Respondents were then asked whether they *strongly agreed, moderately agreed, neither agreed nor disagreed, moderately disagreed,* or *strongly disagreed* with this statement. Her findings revealed that half of the sample either strongly or moderately agreed with the statement and the other half either disagreed or neither agreed nor disagreed. These data showed that the question of language loyalty was somewhat contentious in the community under investigation. In order to find out how people were divided on the issue, she then looked at the numbers, taking two factors into consideration: generation and social class. By generation she found that first- and second-generation respondents were much more likely to agree that Spanish is an important part of being Hispanic. Third-generation respondents, on the other hand, categorically disagreed with the statement. By social class, on the other hand, she found that lower-class respondents were most likely to agree with the statement and that middle- and upper-class respondents were more likely to disagree. These data suggest that Spanish begins to lose its place as an important part of ethnic identity as people become more entrenched in U.S. society, either through length of residence in the country or through more elevated social status as determined by accumulation of wealth (Rivera-Mills 2000, 383).

Margarita Hidalgo reports somewhat contrasting data in her study of the southern California community of Chula Vista. In this community, she studied the contrasting language attitudes of Mexican American adolescents and their parents. In her questionnaire, she presented respondents with three statements that reflect attitudes about language and identity. The three statements were (1) *Spanish is important for speaking like Mexicans,* (2) *Spanish is important for behaving like Mexicans,* and (3) *Spanish is important for preserving Hispanic identity.* Notice that the first two questions call up Mexican identity, whereas the final question uses the more general term *Hispanic.* From the results of Hidalgo's study, this stimulus seemed to be an important element in eliciting language attitudes. Almost all of the parents strongly agreed with item 3 and more than half strongly agreed with items 1 and 2. This pattern shows that for nearly half of the parents in the survey, being Hispanic and speaking and behaving like Mexicans are not the same. The pattern is even more evident when we look at how the adolescents responded to these items: 27 percent strongly agreed with item 1, 18 percent strongly agreed with item 2, and 53 percent strongly agreed with item 3. Here again we see that Mexican identity and Hispanic identity are two very different things in the southern California context and that this difference is more pronounced in the children than in the parents. Hidalgo's data, therefore, seem to indicate that while Spanish is being lost as a marker of Mexican identity, it is being preserved as a marker of Hispanic identity (Hidalgo 1993, 57).

In comparing Rivera-Mills' northern California data with Hidalgo's southern California data, we can see notable differences. These differences may be attributable to the geographic contexts in which the two studies were carried out. Fortuna, the site of the Rivera-Mills study, is located in extreme northern California. Chula Vista, the site of the Hidalgo study, is a suburb of San Diego located seven miles north of the Mexican border and seven miles south of downtown San Diego. The proximity to the border may have been one reason why Hidalgo's respondents differentiated themselves from Mexicans and were more prone to adopt a Hispanic identity. Even so, for them being Hispanic, as opposed to Mexican, still involved speaking Spanish as a defining characteristic. For the northern California respondents, however, the issue of differentiation seemed to be less pressing. The declining importance of Spanish to Hispanic identity among adolescents would seem to reflect a desire among the younger non-Spanish-speaking generations to be considered as a distinctive ethnic group bound together with their Spanish-speaking counterparts.

The role of geography in language attitudes is underscored in another study carried out by John Attinasi in northern Indiana. In his study, Attinasi set out to determine whether or not the values of Hispanics melt into the larger pot of general North American Anglo attitudes as members disperse among other populations in suburbs and small cities. His findings revealed that Mexican Americans in the Midwest were very concerned about the role of the Spanish language in their lives and in the lives of their children. However, when asked about the social implications of not speaking Spanish, they displayed an overwhelming tolerance. Attinasi specifically asked respondents whether they felt that Hispanics who speak only one language divide the community. The respondents chose between four possible answers: (1) *Those who speak only Spanish or only English divide the community,* (2) *Those who speak only English divide the community,* (3) *Those who speak only Spanish divide the community,* (4) *Speaking only one language does not divide the community.* The majority of respondents chose item 4, indicating that the ability to speak only one language was not a divisive factor. Nearly 20 percent indicated that English monolinguals were divisive and only 6 percent felt that Spanish monolinguals were divisive. These data suggest that even though Spanish is not viewed as a necessary component of Hispanic identity and solidarity, it is highly valued within the community. The very low percentage of respondents who feel that Spanish monolinguals divide the community is striking in comparison to the relatively high percentage who feel that English monolinguals are divisive (Attinasi 1985, 48).

Considering these data in tandem with the data from the Hidalgo and Rivera-Mills studies suggests an elevated place for Spanish in the construction of Hispanic identity among Mexican Americans. The Rivera-Mills study suggests that relatively assimilated and socially mobile Mexican Americans deemphasize the role of Spanish in their identity constructs. One of her respondents underscored this sentiment, stating, "When you come to the United States, I think you have to adapt and change. Sometimes that means letting go of other things like language" (Rivera-Mills 2000, 383). Other respondents in her study similarly de-emphasized the role of Spanish in Hispanic identity, as did the second-generation respondent who argued that "you can be Hispanic without speaking the language. There are many Hispanics in the United States who don't speak Spanish and they still consider themselves Hispanic because they continue to have the cultural values and traditions of our culture" (Rivera-Mills 2000, 382). The Attinasi study suggests that while there is a tolerance toward "letting go" of Spanish, there is at the same time a great acceptance of those who "hang on" to Spanish. The same generalization can be drawn from the Hidalgo study. While hanging on to Spanish is not seen as something that necessarily connects respondents to Mexico, it is something that distinguishes them as a distinct group within the United States.

This conclusion is easily drawn from the first longitudinal study of language attitudes in the Mexican American community. This study by Hugo Mejías, Pamela Anderson-Mejías, and Ralph Carlson compared data from a 1982 survey of language attitudes in the lower Rio Grande Valley of Texas with data from a similar 2000 survey. They found that whereas the 1982 respondents were most likely to view Spanish positively because of its communication value, the 2000 respondents were most likely to view it positively because of its value as a marker of group identity (Mejías, Anderson-Mejías, and Carlson 2003, 147). What this means is that even though younger speakers are not using Spanish as much as their parents or grandparents, they are still assigning it considerable importance in locating their identities in the larger U.S. matrix of cultures.

Many scholars have argued that such positive sentiments about Spanish are politically motivated. Joyce Penfield and Jacob Ornstein-Galicia, for instance, argue that "because of the chicanismo movement beginning in the '60's which reacted to cultural domination by Anglos as well as linguistic domination in the form of Standard English, Chicano varieties of English and Spanish came to be viewed as positive markers of cultural identification within the Chicano community as well as a positive indicator of ethnic identity between Chicanos" (Penfield and Ornstein-Galicia 1985, 71). This interpretation underscores the salience of language pride in the community and connects it to a vibrant and viable ideological formation that serves to legitimize and promote the cultural interests of the minority group.

The Rivera-Mills study, however, challenges the political motivation hypothesis by showing that those respondents who are more assimilated and socially mobile also tend to be more politically desensitized when it comes to issues of linguistic rights and cultural entitlements. She found that most of her respondents felt that English should be the official language of the United States and that bilingual education was a waste of time (Rivera-Mills 2000, 384–85). This political desensitization is compounded in the Rivera-Mills study when we consider the adjectives that her respondents generally used to describe other Hispanics. She asked her respondents what adjectives they would use to describe Hispanics in Fortuna and then tallied the results depending on whether the adjectives were positive, negative, or neutral. The tally revealed that 71 percent of the adjectives used were negative and included descriptors such as *flojos* (lazy), *maleducados* (rude) *sin educación* (uneducated), *vividores* (freeloading), and *impermeables* (unassimilable; Rivera-Mills 2000, 385–86). In this study, therefore, we can see that within the minority community there is an oppositional constellation of attitudes that converge on conflicting ideologies of language panic and language pride.

■ Attitudes about Language Variation

In the previous section, we considered several studies on attitudes about language and identity and how they uncovered the tension between language pride and language panic. In this section, we will see that attitudes about language variation can also illuminate the ideological tensions between language pride and language panic that emerge in the Mexican American community. One way of eliciting attitudes about language variation is by asking direct questions about speakers' perceptions of how language varies and what that variation might mean. For instance, we could use a sociolinguistic questionnaire to determine speakers' reactions to a given language variety. In this case, we might ask if a respondent agrees or disagrees with a statement such as, *The Spanish spoken in Brownsville, Texas, is border slang*. Alternatively, we could present the respondent with several options, such as, *The Spanish spoken in Tucson, Arizona, is* (1) *formal educated Spanish,* (2) *informal everyday Spanish,* (3) *Southwest dialect Spanish,* (4) *border slang*.

Attitudes about language variation can also be elicited by determining a listener's response to concrete linguistic facts. This elicitation procedure is often referred to as a **matched-guise test.** Matched-guise tests set out to reveal the extent to which people's speech influences how they are perceived. A matched-guise test normally presents respondents with a set of alternating words or sentences that are equivalent in meaning but different in form. For example, we might present a group of English speakers with sentences such as these:

A		B
I done it yesterday	vs.	*I did it yesterday*
He ain't got it	vs.	*He hasn't got it*
It was her what said it	vs.	*It was she who said it*

Presented with these linguistic options, the respondents would be asked to rate the sentences on some type of scale, such as correct versus incorrect, pleasant versus unpleasant, proper versus improper. We can also extend this evaluation and ask the respondents to rate the speaker not just the form. In this case we would ask the respondents' impressions of speaker A and speaker B using categories such as intelligent versus unintelligent, friendly versus unfriendly, and so on. As we survey further language attitude studies in the Mexican American community, we will see the value of both types of questions (see topic highlight 4).

Norman Binder conducted a study on attitudes about language variation in Brownsville, Texas, in order to determine how respondents viewed the local variety of Spanish. He queried three groups of Spanish-speaking respondents—educators, businesspeople, and other citizens—about how they perceived the Spanish spoken in Brownsville. He gave the respondents five labels to choose from: (1) *formal educated Spanish,* (2) *informal everyday Spanish,* (3) *Southwest Spanish dialect,* (4) *south Texas Spanish dialect,* or (5) *border slang.* He also asked the respondents to characterize the Spanish that they themselves spoke using the same categories. The results of his study demonstrated that educators and businesspeople overwhelmingly characterized Brownsville Spanish as "border slang." Average citizens, on the other hand, tended to characterize Brownsville Spanish as "informal everyday Spanish." In terms of rating their own Spanish, educators and businesspeople were more or less divided between "formal educated Spanish" and "informal everyday Spanish." Average citizens overwhelmingly chose "informal everyday Spanish" to describe their own Spanish (Binder 1989, 167). This study points out a marked polarization in the perception of Spanish in Brownsville. It shows that those groups more familiar with prestige domains for the use of Spanish, the school and the workplace, perceive the local dialect somewhat negatively; however, these speakers do not identify their own speech with this variety. Among the respondents who have less familiarity with prestige domains, the perception of the

Frederick Williams conducted a matched-guise experiment among forty-five undergraduate students at the University of Texas (Williams 1976). He presented the subjects with speech samples in standard English and Spanish-accented English. He then asked the subjects to rate the speaker's personality on a scale of 1 to 7 (where 1 = very much and 7 = very little) in different areas such as sense of humor, kindness, and intelligence. Table 1 gives respondents' average ratings on the different traits. How would you characterize this group's view of standard English speakers and Spanish-accented English speakers? ■

Table 1   Attitudes toward Spanish-accented English

CHARACTERISTIC	STANDARD ENGLISH	SPANISH-ACCENTED ENGLISH
Sense of humor	3.0	4.2
Intelligence	3.9	3.6
Likeability	4.3	5.0
Kindness	4.3	5.1
Sociability	3.3	4.1

Data from Williams 1976

language spoken around them is less negative and more like the perception of their own speech.

Susana Rivera-Mills' study also demonstrates this attitudinal duality. The participants in her study were asked whether the Spanish they spoke at home was better, the same as, or different from the Spanish spoken generally in Fortuna, California. Seventy-five percent of the respondents claimed that the Spanish spoken in their homes was better than the Spanish spoken in the community at large (Rivera-Mills 2000, 381). It is compelling to see the attitudinal duality that emerges when speakers evaluate the speech of their own community and distance themselves from it.

Other attitude studies carried out in the Southwest shed light on the specific features that are associated with this attitudinal duality. Merryl Kravitz conducted a matched-guise experiment with respondents from four communities in New Mexico. He presented respondents with synonymous sentences that contained one alternating element in the areas of **lexicon** (vocabulary), **syntax** (grammar), **morphology** (components of words), and **phonology** (pronunciation).

Lexicon: *Esta maestra sabe tichar* vs. *Esta maestra sabe enseñar*
Syntax: *¿Conoce a la María?* vs. *¿Conoce a María?*
Morphology: *Vuelamos rápido* vs. *Volamos rápido*
Phonology: *¿Ves al mushasho?* vs. *¿Ves al muchacho?*

The alternating elements reflect lexical, syntactic, morphological, and phonological features characteristic of Southwest Spanish contrasted with features more common in standard Mexican Spanish. After presenting each pair to the respondents, Kravitz asked them which sentence in the pair would seem to them to be more "correct" in a formal, educated setting. The responses overwhelmingly favored the standard Mexican Spanish form over the Southwest Spanish form. The data also seemed to indicate, however, that respondents were most aware of lexical differences and least aware of syntactic differences (Kravitz 1989, 153–56). These data seem to suggest, then, that the attitudinal duality noted previously may be grounded in the use of salient lexical items.

Arnulfo Ramírez carried out a similar study among adolescents in San Jose, California, and San Antonio, Texas. In his study, respondents were presented not with pairs of synonymous sentences but rather with four synonymous paragraphs. Each paragraph contained elements of one variety of Spanish. Text 1 displayed code switching discourse, text 2 illustrated nonfluent, ungrammatical Spanish, text 3 contained dialectal variants characteristic of Southwest Spanish, and text 4 represented standard Mexican Spanish. The respondents were asked to evaluate each text on the basis of (1) the usefulness of that variety in the classroom, (2) the grammaticality of the variety, and (3) the academic potential of speakers who use the variety. The adolescents rated text 4—standard Mexican Spanish—as the most useful, the most grammatical, and the one that correlated with the greatest academic potential. Furthermore, they rated text 1—code switching discourse—as the least useful, the least grammatical, and the one that correlated with the least academic potential (Ramírez 1992, 68–73). It is interesting to note that in both the Kravitz study and the Ramírez study, the most negative attitudes were triggered by the presence of English items in Spanish discourse.

These studies would suggest that there is a negative backlash against code switching in the Mexican American community; however, it is important to realize that each of these studies was specifically asking what respondents thought was correct and appropriate in specific formal situations. Other studies on code switching show how Mexican Americans negotiate attitudes about their own bilingual speech and how oppositional attitudes toward code switching filter in from different sources. Carmen Fought, for instance, has demonstrated that code switching is associated with ethnic identity. Many of her respondents viewed Spanish-English code switching as a "normal" part of everyday verbal encounters and transactions (Fought 2003, 208–10). Rosa Fernández similarly found that whereas Mexican American students may judge code switching to be "out of place" in the classroom, they also perceive it as useful and justified in intimate and informal situations (Fernández 1990, 54).

While situation may be an important controlling variable in attitudes toward code switching, some studies suggest that attitudes about code switching intersect with different types of social allegiances. For instance, Norma Mendoza-Denton studied language attitudes among Latina gangs in a California high school. Her data showed a clear division in attitudes about code switching that corresponds with other differences such as style of clothing and academic expectations in school. She identified two types of Latina gangs, Norteñas and Sureñas, and concluded that "for some Latina girls in California, Spanish and English are not neutral media of communication but symbols of social allegiance and identity" (Mendoza-Denton 1999, 41). In particular, she noted that while Sureñas preferred to speak Spanish and disparaged both code switching and the tendency of Norteñas to pretend not to know Spanish, Norteñas tended to speak mostly in English and to code switch with greater frequency (p. 51).

Margarita Hidalgo found residents of the border city of Ciudad Juárez, Chihuahua, south of El Paso, Texas, also tended to disparage code switching as an affront to their identity. "Border residents," she writes, "are aware that the use of 'pure' English does not alter their ethnicity, but they feel that the mixture of the two languages—code-switching—may well infringe upon their identity" (Hidalgo 1984, 29).

These studies show that attitudes about language variation pattern along different axes—the I versus the Other (Rivera-Mills, Binder, Mendoza-

Denton, and Hidalgo) or formal versus informal situations (Kravitz, Ramírez, and Fernández). These attitudes straddle and strain the tensions between the underlying ideological formations in the Mexican American language experience. It would appear that the I/Other axis serves to counter language panic ideologies that would seek to meld all Mexican American verbal activity into one deformed and degenerate variety. At the same time, however, the formal/informal axis serves to buttress language pride ideologies that tolerate the crossing of linguistic boundaries and underscore the reality of living between two languages.

■ Attitudes about Language Maintenance

The tensions between language pride and language prejudice are also evident in attitudes about the importance of keeping Spanish alive. Numerous studies on language attitudes have asked respondents their opinions regarding the future vitality of the Spanish language in the United States. These studies generally show that most respondents are positive about the future viability of the language and that they are to some degree committed to keeping the language alive.

Susana Rivera-Mills, for instance, asked her Fortuna, California, respondents if they felt it was important for them to maintain Spanish. Responses were overwhelmingly affirmative among all respondents. The vast majority of first- and second-generation Latinos were in strong agreement with the statement while more than half of the third-generation respondents strongly agreed as well (Rivera-Mills 2000, 379). Attinasi also asked about language maintenance in his survey. He asked respondents who they felt had the responsibility for maintaining Spanish. His data revealed that while 60 percent felt that the family bears the greatest responsibility for language maintenance, 27 percent felt that language maintenance was the joint responsibility of the family and other social institutions such as churches, civic organizations, and schools. Only 4 percent of the respondents felt that the majority of the responsibility rested on the shoulders of schools (Attinasi 1985, 48). These two studies reveal that while Mexican Americans feel strongly about maintaining the Spanish language, they feel that this responsibility falls more within the boundaries of the family and the wider Mexican American community than within the framework of the public school system (see topic highlight 5).

This general sentiment can also be seen in the fieldwork carried out by

Topic Highlight 5. **Language Attitudes among Bilingual Educators**

Patricia MacGregor-Mendoza (1998) conducted an attitude survey of 77 bilingual teachers in the El Paso–Las Cruces area. Table 2 summarizes the responses. Study the questions and the number of teachers who agreed and disagreed with each one. What do you conclude about the attitudes of these teachers in terms of language and identity and language maintenance? ■

Table 2 Attitude survey of bilingual educators

	STRONGLY AGREE (%)	MOSTLY AGREE (%)	NEUTRAL (%)	MOSTLY DISAGREE (%)	STRONGLY DISAGREE (%)
Bilingual education should teach Latinos Spanish	66	16	12	5	1
Latinos should know Spanish	53	18	25	3	1
Spanish helps the Latino community progress	35	30	26	3	6
Spanish is an important part of Latino culture	65	26	4	4	1

Data from MacGregor-Mendoza 1998.

Sandra Schecter and Robert Bayley in northern California and in San Antonio, Texas. The researchers set out to document what kinds of activities Mexican American families engaged in to maintain the Spanish language. They found three general patterns. First, in some families Spanish was mandated in the home. In these cases, parents normally went out of their way to expose children to numerous activities in Spanish, including reading and writing. The second pattern occurred in homes where Spanish was encouraged. In these cases, parents would seek out opportunities for children to use the language, for instance, by making trips to Mexico or having relatives from Mexico stay with them in their homes, but rarely did they insist that their children speak Spanish. The third pattern emerged in homes where Spanish was reserved for endearment. In these households, most routine conversation was carried out in English, but there was an expectation that acts of endearment should be carried out in Spanish (Schecter and Bayley 2002). These varied approaches to maintaining the language would seem to suggest different levels of commitment to keeping the language alive. In a study of Spanish in Los Angeles, California, Carmen Silva-Corvalán attempted to measure respondents' level of commitment to language maintenance. In her attitude survey, she presented a series of nine yes/no questions such as, *Would you agree to attend a meeting of a local chapter of a Mexican American organization for the strengthening of the use of Spanish in Los Angeles?* and *Would you, if asked, contribute $15.00 to help finance the activities of a Mexican American organization for the strengthening of the use of Spanish in Los Angeles?* The number of "yes" responses to these questions indicated the level of commitment to Spanish maintenance. The tally of responses revealed that first-generation Mexican Americans were more committed to maintaining the language than third-generation respondents. Silva-Corvalán (1994, 203–5) concludes that even though most Mexican Americans express positive attitudes about Spanish language maintenance, these positive attitudes do not translate into action to support Spanish. This contradiction would seem to be another manifestation of the tension between the ideologies of language pride and language panic.

◼ Concluding Thoughts

In this chapter we have looked at the distinction between language ideologies and language attitudes, suggesting that attitudes are the individual components of language ideologies. We then surveyed a series of attitude studies involving the Mexican American community and saw how these individual attitudes conflate into an overarching ideological tension between language pride and language panic. We viewed the presence of language pride and language panic in attitudes about language and identity, about language variation, and about language maintenance. In each of these areas opposing attitudes revealed tensions between the absence or presence of Spanish as an identity marker, between standard Spanish and English-inflected Spanish, and between the desire to maintain Spanish and the commitment to enact that maintenance. Such oppositions show how the I and the Other intersect with community and individuality and, thus, unfold in a basic ideological tension between language pride and language panic.

■ Discussion Exercises

1. Consider the following list of questions. Indicate which attitudinal dimension the responses might elucidate: communication, instrumentalism, loyalty, or sentimentalism.
   a. I use Spanish to feel good about myself.
   b. I use Spanish because it helps me make money at work.
   c. I use Spanish to keep my traditional values.
   d. I use Spanish to communicate with my grandma.

2. How do language ideologies differ from language attitudes?

3. Explain the difference between overt and covert prestige.

4. Draft a question you might include in a sociolinguistic questionnaire in order to determine attitudes about language and identity. What would you hope to find out through this question?

5. Describe the matched-guise experiment and how it is used to uncover attitudes about language variation.

6. What kind of question would you ask in order to determine attitudes about language maintenance? How would you modify this question in order to determine commitment to language maintenance?

7. Conduct a survey of attitudes about language maintenance in your community. Choose three bilingual Latinas/os who have children over the age of

twelve, three who have children under the age of twelve, and three who have no children. Ask each person to respond to the following statements with strongly agree, somewhat agree, neither agree nor disagree, somewhat disagree, or strongly disagree:

a. It is important for my children to be able to speak Spanish.
b. Parents should force children to speak Spanish in the home.
c. Parents should send their children to schools where some instruction is given in Spanish.
d. Parents should encourage children to watch TV in Spanish.

Do Latinas/os who have children view language maintenance differently than those who do not? Do you see any difference among those parents whose children are older and those whose children are younger?

Suggested Readings

Baker, Colin. *Attitudes and Language*. Clevedon, U.K.: Multilingual Matters, 1992.

Niedzielski, Nancy A., and Dennis R. Preston. *Folk Linguistics*. Berlin: Mouton de Gruyter, 2003.

Peñalosa, Fernando. *Chicano Sociolinguistics*. Rowley, MA: Newbury House, 1980.

Schecter, Sandra, and Robert Bayley. *Language as Cultural Practice*. Mahwah, NJ: Lawrence Erlbaum, 2002.

3

Language Maintenance and Shift

In the last two chapters, we have been considering the basic ideological tension between language pride and language panic in the Mexican American **language experience.** In chapter 1, I argued that this tension is born out of the contradictory ideas and values about language routinely experienced in the United States. On the one hand, there is the experience of the supremacy of English and the elevation of whiteness, which is actualized in concrete social and political acts that diminish the value of Mexican American language. On the other hand, the persistent use of Spanish, both in the home and outside of it, continually transgresses these concrete social and political acts of English supremacy. In chapter 2, I continued my analysis of this basic tension by showing how language attitudes within the Mexican American community can oftentimes exemplify both ideologies at the same time.

In this chapter we will go beyond the attitudinal dimensions of this ideological tension and study how it interfaces with the lived experiences of Mexican Americans throughout the United States. What effect do language attitudes have on language use? How do such changes in language use interrupt family life and family values? Why do these changes continue even while they pose such a serious threat to the perceived well-being of the community? (See topic highlight 6.)

■ Language Shift

In this chapter, we will study the multiple dimensions of **language shift** in the Mexican American community. Language shift refers to a process in which a community completely gives up one language in favor of another (Fasold 1987, 213). This definition of language shift highlights two very important facts about the process that we must keep in mind. The definition specifies that language shift is always community based not individually based. While it is certainly possible, and in fact quite common, that an individual will learn one language as a child and gradually shift to another one throughout the course of his or her life, we would not use *language shift* to refer to this process. In this case we would speak instead of **language attrition.** Language attrition is an individual phenomenon that occurs when a person stops using a language and thus begins to forget something of its structure or vocabulary. Language attrition occurs because the occasions and opportunities an individual encounters for using a given language have contracted or become restricted in some way. Language attrition does not, however, normally refer to complete loss of a language, for even if someone seldom uses a language, the tacit knowledge of the language, even if it is somewhat flawed, normally lies nascent in the individual's mind. Language shift, on the other hand, does refer to complete loss of the language. Because of this, some have used the phrase *language death* to refer to this process.

In order for a language to die, its speakers must in some way cease to exist. Because of this, language shift is always a generational process where one generation fails to pass the language on to the next. It is uncommon that language shift should occur from one generation to the next. The normal cycle of language death is that a language is transmitted in decreasing degrees over a period of several generations. We can think about decreasing degrees of transmission as a situation in which the **functional domains** reserved for one language are overtaken by another language. For instance, one generation may use a certain language for religious practices and events and in the home. A subsequent generation relinquishes use of the language in the home but maintains it in religious practices and events. A final generation relinquishes the language in religious domains and the shift is now complete because the terminal generation no longer uses the language. The language has become obsolete.

In order to understand how a language becomes obsolete over a period of generations, we must make a distinction between bilingualism—the knowledge and use of two languages—and **diglossia**—the social norms that dictate the functional distribution of those two languages in communicative practices. Diglossia may be viewed as regulating bilingualism. Different diglossic situations, in effect, determine the degree to which a language is susceptible to shift and consequently the degree to which bilingualism is susceptible to obsolescence.

We might think of a situation where all members of a speech community are bilingual. These members are also aware of the appropriate functions of each language, so they would never use language A in domain B or language B in domain A. Such a situation could be characterized as **stable bilingualism** because as long as the diglossic situations remain intact, the two languages do not come into direct competition.

A different situation might occur in which a large proportion of the members of a speech community are bilingual but the social norms that govern the use of one language or the other are not fixed. Instead, speakers choose which language to use on the basis of individual preferences and communicative demands. Such a situation could be characterized as **dynamic bilingualism** because the diglossic situation itself is unable to prevent the two languages from coming into direct competition. Dynamic bilingualism may last for many generations; however, it always opens the door to the possibility of language shift. Dynamic bilingualism, for instance, can lead to a situation in which, for a variety of idiosyncratic reasons, speakers begin to choose language A much more often than language B in domains that were once reserved for language B.

Once this process begins to unfold in a progressive and general way, there is a situation of **transitional bilingualism** in which one language systematically loses its domains of use. Transitional bilingualism can often

Table 3 Language choice by age and interlocutor

What language do you use when speaking to ...	SPEAKER NUMBER AND AGE					
	1 (AGE 14)	3 (AGE 25)	8 (AGE 39)	14 (AGE 40)	17 (AGE 50)	28 (AGE 71)
God	H	H	H	H	H	H
Grandparents	GH	GH	H	H	H	H
Parents	G	GH	H	H	H	H
Neighbors	G	G	GH	H	H	H
Siblings	G	G	GH	H	H	H
Salespeople	G	G	G	H	H	H
Spouse	—	G	G	GH	H	H
Children	—	G	G	GH	H	H
Government officials	G	G	G	GH	H	H
Doctors	G	G	G	G	G	H

G = German   H = Hungarian   GH = both German and Hungarian
Data from Gal 1979, 121.

be gauged by determining the language choices of individual speakers from different generations. Susan Gal (1979) uncovered a situation of transitional bilingualism in Oberwart, Austria. She demonstrated how a long-standing situation of bilingualism between German and Hungarian was undergoing language shift. She asked a group of bilingual women between the ages of fourteen and seventy-one to indicate which language—Hungarian (H), German (G), or both (GH)—they would use in different situations. Table 3 partially summarizes Gal's findings. As we can see, German is progressively encroaching on all domains for the youngest speakers but the oldest speakers maintain Hungarian in all domains. From these data it is patently obvious that within a matter of generations Hungarian will have become obsolete in this speech community. Once a language reaches the point of obsolescence, however, traces of it, such as the occasional use of isolated words and phrases, oftentimes survive for many subsequent generations. This situation is referred to as **vestigial bilingualism**—when fragments of a language persist with no real communicative value. Vestigial bilingualism is common in many Mexican American communities in the Southwest. Margarito Garza's comic book *Relampago*

■ 3. Margarito Garza's comic book hero Relampago demonstrates vestigial bilingualism through the use of sparsely interspersed, emblematic Spanish words. (Courtesy of Mrs. Caroline Garza)

illustrates the occasional use of interspersed, isolated words and phrases (see figure 3).

■ Motivations for Language Shift

Now that we have reviewed how language shift progresses through different distributional patterns of appropriate and preferred language use, we can ask why such distributional patterns should change in the first place. Ethnolinguistic vitality is a theory that seeks to explain the survival or demise of languages in competition. Giles, Bourhis, and Taylor (1977, 307) define ethnolinguistic vitality as "that which makes a group likely to behave as a distinctive and active collective entity in intergroup relations." Low vitality favors greater convergence with the dominant group and ultimately results in language shift whereas high vitality favors greater divergence from the dominant group and ultimately leads to **language maintenance.** The research of Howard Giles and associates has shown that by attending to different structural variables in a given society, it is possible to determine the level of ethnolinguistic vitality in minority language communities. These structural variables are grouped under three broad headings: status, demography, and institutional support.

Economic, social, sociohistorical, and linguistic factors influence the status of an ethnolinguistic group within a given society. The economic factor refers to the relative control a group has over the economic life of the community. A minority community that is composed largely of merchants and landowners will often carry high economic status whereas a group that is composed mostly of laborers will have low economic status.

Social status is measured in terms of the degree of esteem that a group has for itself. Social status is thus intimately tied to the level of pride that the group has in itself as a separate collective entity. It is important to note that "often self-esteem closely resembles that attributed it by the outgroup" (Giles, Bourhis, and Taylor 1977, 310). Nowhere is this more evident than in Lambert's study of language attitudes in Quebec (cited in Grosjean 1982). The results of this study revealed that "the negative attitudes of the majority group toward the group without power and prestige are adopted in part or in whole by this group, and are often amplified to such an extent that members of the minority group downgrade themselves even more than they are downgraded by the dominant group" (p. 119).

Sociohistorical status is determined by the remembered historical events that inspire individuals to bind together as a group. A group with high sociohistorical sensitivity makes a concerted effort to transmit the cultural and historical heritage of the group from generation to generation.

Linguistic status is defined by Giles and associates in terms of the international prestige a language itself is seen to have. Thus, minority groups in Quebec and in the U.S. Southwest have a higher linguistic status than, for instance, minority groups in Oaxaca, Mexico, because French and Spanish are seen as languages with international prestige while Mixteco, Zapoteco, and Popoluca are not. Yet Haarmann (1986) has criticized the formulation of this variable as much too broad to yield any significant explanatory value in the measurement of ethnolinguistic vitality. The fact that a language carries international prestige in an area that is far removed from the ethnolinguistic minority has little bearing on the status of the minority language. Indeed, it seems that the very fact that an internationally acknowledged variety (such as Castilian Spanish) is spoken in some part of the world may play a part in assigning an even lower status to the minority variety (such as U.S. Southwest Spanish). If the minority variety diverges from the standard variety, this often provides an opportunity for the dominant group to downgrade the subordinate group in opposition to the "true speakers" of the language.

Demographic variables are other contributing factors to the relative ethnolinguistic vitality of a minority language group. The distribution of the group members over a given geographic region is particularly important to the evaluation of ethnolinguistic vitality. When the minority group perceives that the territory it occupies is an ethnolinguistic homeland, as opposed to a foreign land, there is a higher likelihood that the group will maintain its vitality as a collective entity. Similarly, group concentration also plays an important role in determining a minority group's ethnolinguistic vitality. "Minority group speakers who concentrate in the same geographic area may stand a better chance of surviving as a dynamic linguistic group" (Giles, Bourhis, and Taylor 1977, 313).

Distribution and concentration may, however, become confounded by group proportion. When the minority group becomes seriously outnumbered, it has little chance of maintaining a high level of ethnolinguistic vitality regardless of whether it perceives the territory as a homeland or is concentrated in dense pockets throughout the area. Thus, the absolute number of the minority language population contributes to higher levels of ethnolinguistic vitality.

Mixed marriages reduce the overall level of ethnolinguistic vitality in the minority language group as well. When the rate of exogamy (marriage outside the group) is great, vitality is usually low, and when the rate of endogamy (marriage within the group) is great, vitality is usually high. Giles and associates (1977, 314) note that "the high status variety has a better chance of surviving as the language of the home, and hence of child rearing, than the low status variety. Subordinate groups then are likely to have more vitality . . . when the incidence of ethnolinguistically mixed marriages is low."

Immigration patterns can also influence the level of vitality through diversification of the group. A homogeneous group is likely to have high vitality while a heterogeneous group is likely to have low vitality. Immigration affects the homogeneity of the group because "migrants who move into an area where linguistic groups are in overt or covert competition appear to be willing to adopt the language and culture of the dominant group rather than that of the subordinate group" (Giles, Bourhis, and Taylor 1977, 314). Therefore, massive immigration, even from similar groups, can threaten the vitality of the ethnolinguistic minority.

■ 4. The Mexican Cultural Center of South Texas serves as a strong informal institutional support for continued Spanish language use while it promotes Mexican music, art, and literature. (Photograph by Glenn Martínez)

Informal institutional support refers to the extent to which a minority group has organized itself in distinction to the dominant group. This self-organization may take such forms as trade unions established along ethnic lines or of patriotic clubs and organizations. The Mexican Cultural Center in south Texas, for example, serves as a strong informal institutional support that, while promoting Mexican music, art, and literature also promotes continued Spanish language use (see figure 4). Media outlets controlled from within the minority language community also constitute an important informal institutional support. Charles Tatum (2001, 89) argues that "Spanish-language newspapers in the Southwest have been at the forefront nationally in helping preserve the Spanish language and Mexican and Mexican American cultural identity in the face of an Anglo culture that became more aggressive after 1848."

Formal institutional support refers to the extent to which minority language groups are represented in the mainstream public affairs of politics, education, and commerce. "Of crucial importance for the vitality of ethnolinguistic groups is the use of the minority language in the state education system at primary, secondary, and higher levels" (Giles, Bourhis, and Taylor 1977, 316). Formal institutional support may also be afforded to a minority language group through religious institutions. The degree to which the minority language is used in religious institutions reveals the level of legitimacy it has attained in the face of the dominant language. Landry and Bourhis argue that the degree to which the minority language appears on public signs in a given region can also reveal the level of legitimacy it has attained. The languages used on commercial and governmental public signs are referred to as the linguistic landscape. The linguistic landscape in downtown McAllen, Texas, reveals widespread use of both English and Spanish on commercial signs (see figure 5). Landry and Bourhis (1997, 26) propose that "the configuration of languages present in the linguistic landscape . . . can provide important information about the diglossic nature of a particular bilingual or multilingual setting. Thus, before communicating interpersonally with a single inhabitant, one can use the linguistic landscape as an indicator of the power and status relationship that exists between the in-group and the out-group." The Landry and Bourhis study revealed that the more a language appears on public signs, the more likely it is to be used in certain domains, especially within commercial and public institutions.

June Jaramillo uses ethnolinguistic vitality measures as an indicator of the relative status and prognosis of the Spanish language in the U.S. Southwest (Jaramillo 1995). Focusing on the Tucson, Arizona, Spanish-speaking community, Jaramillo suggests that the overall ethnolinguistic vitality among Mexican Americans is low. She ranks status variables as low on the basis of the professional status of the workforce, the linguistic status of the language, and in-group solidarity and out-group perceptions. The Mexican American workforce in Tucson is composed predominantly of non-professional, unskilled workers. This results in an extremely low level of socioeconomic status. In-group identity and pride, on the other hand, seem to be quite high, given the long-standing tradition of residence in the area. At the same time, however, this in-group solidarity is attenuated by the out-group's (Anglos') perceptions of the Mexican American community. The Spanish language itself enjoys high status as the national language of the neighboring nation. Furthermore, "there is emerging evidence that Spanish in the area is also deriving societal prestige due to various demo-

■ 5. The linguistic landscape of downtown McAllen, Texas, reveals widespread use of both English and Spanish. (Photo by Glenn Martínez)

graphic, political, and economic motivations" (Jaramillo 1995, 86). Institutional support variables, on the other hand, were ambivalent in the Tucson community. Even though English has received protected status under Arizona law, Spanish language use seems to be pervasive in educational, commercial, media, and religious institutions. The Mexican American intelligentsia and politicians are increasingly mobilizing to maintain and promote Spanish language use in governmental institutions. Demographic variables were ranked low in Jaramillo's study because Mexican Americans constitute only one-fourth of the region's population. In spite of the relatively low demographic representation of Mexican Americans in the Tucson area, however, the spatial link provided by proximity to Mexico led Jaramillo to propose that these numbers are more likely to increase than to decrease. The net gain in population will be a crucial determining factor in the resurgence of ethnolinguistic vitality in Tucson, Arizona.

Ethnolinguistic vitality is a robust theory of the social motivations of language shift. While it may seem somewhat deterministic in that certain configurations of social factors appear to be inextricably linked to particular language behaviors, its force and focus are rather on the ways that these social factors impinge on the degree and variety of language input that speakers are exposed to and the substantive opportunities they have to speak the language. In other words, language maintenance or language shift boils down to the degree to which speakers are learning the language. If speakers have little exposure to the language and are seldom required to use it, it will surely fade into obsolescence over time.

■ Language Shift in the Mexican American Community

Studies of language maintenance and language shift in the Mexican American community have consistently found clear patterns of loss of the Spanish language over time. The studies have looked at large samples collected from official U.S. Census records and at smaller samples using more elaborate questionnaires. These studies have shown that Mexican Americans display a general tendency to give up use of Spanish in the home, that Spanish proficiency among Mexican Americans is decreasing at a very fast pace, and that maintenance of Spanish correlates generally with social and economic disenfranchisement.

In an early, small-scale study of the Albuquerque, New Mexico, barrio of Martineztown, Hudson-Edwards and Bills (1980, 156) found that within the Mexican American households studied, "each successive generation showed increasingly Anglophone traits." Their survey revealed striking differences between parents and children in the barrio. Whereas 95 percent of the parent generation claimed Spanish as their "mother tongue," only 50 percent of the child generation made the same claim. Similarly, whereas 85 percent of parents felt themselves to be fluent Spanish speakers only 33 percent of children claimed fluency in the language. Based on these data, the authors conclude that the younger generation tended not to develop "mature native speaker competence" in Spanish even though it was their mother tongue, or the first language they learned. They also noted that the younger generations tended to resort to the use of English as a primary language of the home even if they had a fluent command of

Spanish. The Martineztown study thus showed that even in what is normally considered a closed ethnic enclave, the power of English to invade functional domains in the home is undeniable.

Bernal-Enríquez (2000) also studied patterns of language shift in New Mexico. Her study focused on the relative degree of proficiency in Spanish among *nuevomexicanos,* specifically on how proficiency levels in Spanish patterned along variables such as age, language spoken in the home, age of English acquisition, and years of schooling. She found that proficiency levels were high among those who claimed to speak only Spanish at home as children but much lower among those who claimed to speak both Spanish and English at home during childhood. Along the same lines, she found that those respondents who had acquired English in the preschool years reported the lowest proficiency levels in Spanish. These data confirm that when English penetrates the home, the subsequent development of Spanish is seriously hindered. Mary Beth Floyd conducted a similar study in Colorado and found that English had nearly ousted Spanish from the home environment. Among her respondents, 74 percent reported not using any Spanish when speaking with parents and 85 percent reported using only English when speaking to siblings. More strikingly, she found that parents themselves overwhelmingly reported using English alone when speaking with their children, even though they often spoke Spanish with each other. These data lead her to suggest that "it is more appropriate for us to speak in terms of language loss than of language maintenance" (Floyd 1982, 302).

Another study by Garland Bills, Alan Hudson, and Eduardo Hernández-Chávez (2000) based on 1990 census data suggests that the incursion of English into the home environment is a phenomenon that emerges in the first generation of immigrants. They concluded that the "process of anglicization begins immediately upon immigration to the U.S. despite the stability seemingly reflected in the data on Spanish use in the home, and that it continues unabated until maximizing after a period of three decades or so" (p. 15). This conclusion is supported by the fact that all age groups in their sample claimed Spanish as the language of the home. When these data were compared to the English proficiency assessments, however, even though the younger respondents were claiming Spanish as the language of the home, they also claimed high levels of proficiency in English. Each of these studies suggests that the incursion of English into the home is patent and that it may be accelerating an already ongoing process of language shift.

While the home has been clearly identified as the most critical site of English incursion into the Mexican American community, many studies have argued that socioeconomic factors may mitigate the ultimate outcome of English penetration. In particular, the data analyzed by Bills, Hudson, and Hernández-Chávez have shown that there is a very direct correlation between socioeconomic status and language maintenance and shift. "Economic status is a strong determinant of language maintenance and language shift," they argue, "the lower the economic status, the greater the use of Spanish, and conversely, the higher the economic status, the higher the proficiency in English and the less extensively is Spanish likely to be used" (Bills, Hudson, and Hernández-Chávez 2000, 25). The authors present compelling data in support of this conclusion. For instance, they show that those respondents who reported the highest levels of proficiency in English also had the highest levels of educational attainment. Those who reported speaking English very well had completed an average of 11.06 years of schooling while those who reported an inability to speak English had completed an average of only 4.79 years of schooling.

A more extensive study conducted by the same researchers bore out this conclusion. In this study, the authors applied four measures of language maintenance and shift to the 1990 census data of the five-state Southwest region. The "count" measure tallied the raw numbers of Spanish home language claimants in each county in the five-state area. The "density" measure tallied the number of Spanish home language claimants as a proportion of the total county population. The "loyalty" measure identified the proportion of Spanish home language claimants in relation to the Hispanic-origin population within a given county, and the "retention" measure was determined by calculating the ratio of loyalty among five- to seventeen-year-olds versus those eighteen and older within a given county. This ratio was intended to measure "the stability of Spanish language claiming across the two age groups and, as such, [to] simulate the transmission of Spanish across generations" (Hudson, Hernández-Chávez, and Bills 1995, 167). Their analysis of these four measures indicated that higher densities of Spanish speakers are disproportionately found in counties with poorer and less well-educated citizens, and that higher educational levels correlate with lower loyalty and retention rates for Spanish (see topic highlight 7).

Topic Highlight 7. Poverty as a Factor in Spanish Language Maintenance

In *Mexican Americans and the U.S. Economy,* Arturo González writes:

> Evidence suggests that improving the educational level of Mexican Americans is one of the most effective ways to reduce the wage gap between them and non-Mexican-origin workers. Improved English language proficiency will also reduce wage differentials, but this variable is highly correlated with education levels. At the same time, maintenance of Spanish may result in highly sought after bilingual workers; these workers may experience labor market rewards that are generally not available to monolingual English speakers. (González 2002, 122)

Compare this statement with the assessment of Hudson, Hernández-Chávez, and Bills:

> The disproportionate representation of Spanish claiming communities in the lower socioeconomic strata of American society may to some degree safeguard them against the full effects of linguistic assimilation, but to the extent that they gain more open access to quality education, to political power and to economic prosperity, they will do so, it seems at the price of the maintenance of Spanish, even in the home domain. (Hudson, Hernández-Chávez, and Bills 1995, 182)

Are the two outlooks in agreement or disagreement? Which assessment do you agree with? Why? ■

Language Shift and Immigration: Illusion or Infusion?

The study of language shift in the Mexican American community is ever mindful of the impact of immigration from Mexico and other Latin American countries on the continued maintenance of the Spanish language.

Hudson, Hernández-Chávez, and Bills (1995, 182) state that "maintenance of Spanish in the Southwest . . . is heavily dependent upon a steady transfusion of speakers from Mexico to communities in the United States, and offer[s] no warrant for the survival of Spanish beyond a point when such speakers are no longer available to replace speakers north of the border lost through mortality or linguistic assimilation." This deterministic view of the role of immigrants in Spanish language maintenance among Mexican Americans is commonplace in the literature. Many scholars, in fact, have argued that the persistence of Spanish among Mexican Americans is largely illusory. Portes and Rumbaut (1996, 218) report "that the appearance of high language loyalty among Mexican Americans is due largely to the effect of continuing high immigration from the country of origin." In this final section of the chapter, I consider the effects of immigration on language maintenance and shift among Mexican Americans.

Some scholars see the role of immigration as a compensatory phenomenon where every Mexican American who loses Spanish is matched by an incoming immigrant for whom it is a first language. This compensatory view generally proposes a three-generation cycle for Spanish in the Southwest in which Mexican Americans are predicted to lose the Spanish language over the course of three generations. At the same time, however, the cycle is overlaid with successive waves of immigration from Mexico. This overlap creates the illusion that successive generations of Mexican Americans are maintaining the language when in fact they are actually just coinciding with a different wave of first-generation immigrants. This "illusion" approach to the study of language maintenance and shift in the Mexican American community is problematic on a number of levels. First of all, it assumes that the generational layers are independent of one another. Second, it aligns generational members into strict and overly deterministic patterns of language behavior.

The approach currently being explored offers a different perspective on the impact of immigration on language maintenance and shift. Instead of viewing immigrant newcomers as surrogate speakers who fill the void left by those Mexican Americans who have abandoned Spanish, this approach perceives a more dynamic role for immigrants in U.S. society. Rather than creating an illusion of language maintenance, immigrants, through interaction and interchange with native-born generations, create a complex infusion of language and culture back into the rapidly shifting second and third generations. In this section, we will consider three models of infusion that attempt to capture the complex ways that immigrants counteract ongoing processes of language shift within and across generations. The first model is based on the notion of **recontact,** the second is grounded in a **social network** framework, and the third takes a **linguistic capital** perspective.

Recontact is a language phenomenon that fundamentally interrupts language shift. Rene Cisneros and Elizabeth Leone describe it as a "continuing relationship between early settlers, their descendants, and recent arrivals that demonstrates the possible influence one group may have on the other with respect to perception of community language experiences and the cultural traditions used by members of the community" (Cisneros and Leone 1983, 185). Recontact, then, is interaction between speakers at different points in the process of language shift that can result in a reversal and a rethreading of the process itself. The presence of recent arrivals from Mexico within Mexican American communities creates a milieu that gives new impetus for reclaiming once rejected language practices. Gilda Ochoa, in her recent study of the La Puente barrio in Los Angeles, argues that the Spanish language is one of the strongest solidarity symbols in the community. Furthermore, she shows how the interactions among early settlers, their descendants, and recent arrivals are continually leading to renewed interest in maintaining and reacquiring the language. Mary Marquez, one of Ochoa's respondents, remarks,

> I notice that in this neighborhood, if you are Spanish-speaking, you would get along a lot better and just feel more comfortable. I feel uncomfortable because of that. The only reason I feel comfortable is because I've lived here all my life and I feel like, "Hey, this is my place." If I just moved here and I spoke English, I'd probably feel a little bit more self-conscious or afraid of my neighbors. (Ochoa 2004, 151)

Mary's comments underscore the ways that recent arrivals have changed her attitudes about the Spanish language. Other La Puente residents have responded to the increasing presence of Spanish in more proactive ways. David Galvez comments,

> I think the language is the most important thing because when you lose the language, you kind of lose hopes of retaining anything. If you have the

language then everything else is out there for you to grasp onto, like food. My son loves Spanish music. So the language is really important for me. If he maintains it, he can seek out everything else and communicate amongst Mexicans when he grows up. (p. 154)

David's remarks show just how powerful the presence of recent arrivals can be for those who are in the process of language shift. His resolute determination to teach his son Spanish is evidence of the influential interactions that arise out of recontact between established U.S. residents and recent arrivals.

Social network approaches to Spanish language maintenance and shift seek to identify and explain how speakers reactivate their knowledge of the shifting language through interactions with Spanish-dominant and monolingual speakers. Social networks can be described as the sum of interpersonal ties among individuals in a social arena. Some ties are very strong, such as those that exist between immediate family members, close friends, and lovers. Other ties are weak and often mediated through a variety of individuals. A social network approach to language maintenance and shift would attempt to determine the effects of strong and weak ties in reversing and reactivating the shifting language.

Holly Cashman approached Spanish language maintenance and shift in Detroit from a social network perspective. Cashman examined the degree of language shift in the community by eliciting different variables that are grounded in speakers' social networks. One variable that she described as "latinidad" consisted of the number of network ties that the respondent identified as Latina/o. A second variable consisted of the number of network ties that the respondent identified as Spanish monolingual. Her findings revealed that among first-generation Detroit residents, individual variables such as age on arrival to the United States correlated most significantly with self-reported Spanish use. Among second-generation residents, however, network variables were by far the most significant. Second-generation residents whose network ties were predominantly Spanish monolingual were more likely to use Spanish. In addition, "the higher the percentage of an informant's network ties that are Latina/o, the more Spanish she or he is likely to use" (Cashman 2001, 84).

Linguistic capital approaches to language maintenance and shift under-

Topic Highlight 8. Spanish as Linguistic Capital

Ofelia García (1995, 153–54) reports that Mexican Americans who claim to speak only English earn an average of $5,761 more than those who claim to speak Spanish only. She also notes that Mexican Americans who claim to be bilingual earn an average of $3,928 *less* than those who claim to be monolingual in English. Do these data support added economic value and enhanced marketability for those Mexican Americans who maintain or reacquire Spanish? In light of these data, why do you think people perceive knowing Spanish as an economic advantage? ■

score the social and economic impacts of immigrant presence in a community. These impacts are perceived as capital that can be of value to the speaker and thus indirectly affect ongoing processes of language shift (see topic highlight 8). A print advertisement for the telemarketing company Convergys highlights this perceived capital in the incentives it offers for bilingual customer service representatives (see figure 6). In assessing the language situation among Mexican Americans in southern California, Maryellen García reports greater economic value associated with Spanish now than in the past. She reminisces of her childhood in Los Angeles, commenting that "at the time when I was growing up, you didn't speak Spanish at all outside of the home" (García 2003, 2). Now, she argues, Spanish is a necessity in Los Angeles. "The pervasiveness of Spanish speakers in the county appears to be revitalizing the language, potentially to the point of reversing the language shift of earlier decades. For example, even though third- and fourth-generation Mexican Americans are now practically English monolingual, the new immigration of Spanish speakers is creating a new demand for professionals fluent in Spanish" (p. 17). García's argument, then, points out the fact that the reversal of language shift among second- and third-generation Mexican Americans initiated by recent immigrants is not confined to symbolic solidarity and social networks but also includes tangible new possibilities for increasing marketability, economic worth, and upward mobility.

6. A print advertisement for a telemarketing firm illustrates the concept of linguistic capital. The company offers attractive incentives for bilingual customer service representatives. (Courtesy of Convergys)

Concluding Thoughts

In this chapter we have explored language shift in the Mexican American community. Language shift is a community process that occurs over generations and is motivated by an interaction of social factors that interfere with the successful transmission of the language from one generation to the next. All of the studies we reviewed on language shift in the Mexican American community indicate that there is an ongoing process of shift in the community that penetrates well into the home environment. We also saw that those communities mostly likely to retain Spanish also tend to be the most socioeconomically disadvantaged.

On the other hand, we concluded our study by considering the multiple ways in which sustained immigration from Mexico is changing this bleak outlook for Spanish maintenance. We saw that the infusion of Spanish monolingual immigrants in Mexican American communities is having tangible effects in interrupting and reversing ongoing language shift. The factors driving this reversal are an increasing sense of solidarity among Mexicans and Mexican Americans, new social networks that include Spanish monolinguals, and the heightened social and economic value of the language associated with the buying power of Spanish speakers in the United States.

Discussion Exercises

1. What is the difference between language shift and language attrition?

2. How does dynamic bilingualism differ from stable bilingualism? Why does dynamic bilingualism increase the probability of future language shift?

3. What is ethnolinguistic vitality and how is it measured?

4. The home is often considered the safest place for minority languages to thrive. What data support the contention that English has already begun to penetrate the Mexican American home?

5. How does immigration affect the ongoing processes of language shift from Spanish to English in the United States?

6. Explain how theories of recontact, social networks, and linguistic capital

offer a richer perspective of the relationship between immigration and language maintenance and shift in the Mexican American community.

■ Suggested Readings

Crystal, David. *Language Death*. Cambridge: Cambridge University Press, 2000.

Gal, Susan. *Language Shift: Social Determinants of Linguistic Change in Bilingual Austria*. New York: Academic Press, 1979.

Ochoa, Gilda. *Becoming Neighbors in a Mexican American Community: Power, Conflict, and Solidarity*. Austin: University of Texas Press, 2004.

Veltman, Calvin. *The Future of the Spanish Language in the United States*. New York: Hispanic Policy Development Project, 1988.

4

Mexican American Spanish

We have examined language perceptions in detail in chapters 1 and 2. Now we turn our attention to the language characteristics that mark these perceptions. As suggested in previous chapters, the language features themselves and the way those features are perceived do not always correspond (see topic highlight 9). Thus, even though people may perceive Mexican American Spanish as a single dialect, there is also a great deal of variety within it—so much variety, in fact, that it might be more accurate to talk about Mexican American Spanishes instead of Mexican American Spanish. In this chapter we will consider the plurality of Mexican American Spanish and the multiple ways in which that plurality both affects and is affected by the social environment of its speakers.

■ Language Variation

All language is inherently variable. While speakers must adhere to certain patterns of uniformity in order to get a message across, they may also introduce numerous variable features without compromising the communicative outcome. Variable language features can involve words, sounds, or grammatical structures. Consider the following examples of language variation:

The *rubber band* broke as	vs.	The *gum band* broke as
I pulled it back.		I pulled it back.
I've got an *idea*.	vs.	I've got an *idear*.
You *are* funny.	vs.	You funny.

Each pair of phrases conveys an identical meaning but the way that the meaning is expressed differs. In the first pair, we see an example of lexical variation where the word *gum band* may be substituted for the word *rubber band*. In the second pair, we find a pronunciation difference where an extra [r] is pronounced at the end of the word *idea*. In the third pair, we find an alternation in the grammatical structure involving the expression of the verb *to be.* This type of language variation can be explained in various ways. The difference between *rubber band* and *gum band* reflects a regional difference, as does the difference between *idea* and *idear.* The difference between *you are funny* and *you funny* reflects an ethnic difference where the latter variant, *you funny,* is commonly associated with African American varieties of English.

Linguists have traditionally demonstrated great interest in both the patterns and the motivations of language variation. The earliest approaches to language variation in the linguistic sciences tended to focus on studying the different words, sounds, and grammatical constructions used in different regions. This type of study allowed linguists to create dialect maps that identified various regional groupings within a predetermined geographic area. The identification of regional speech patterns led to the idea of the speech community. A speech community refers to a group of speakers sharing a geographic space and certain linguistic characteristics.

Alternative approaches to language variation soon challenged the notion of the speech community, recognizing that even within a particular geographic area, considerable language variation was still evident. In these alternative approaches, language variation was seen as a reflection or an index of social variation. So, a linguist taking such an approach to language variation would attempt to correlate linguistic features with relatively static social categories such as age, sex, social class, and ethnicity. These approaches to language variation demonstrated that linguistic features are reflective of different social categories: teenagers versus adults, men versus women, and middle-class versus working-class speakers all tend to prefer different language forms. In a sense, these different language forms are a component of the social categories they reflect. In sum, whereas early approaches to language variation attempted to identify language variation across speech communities, more recent approaches have sought to identify language variation within a speech community.

As linguists interested in language variation have continued researching different speech communities, however, they have started to notice that even within a social grouping inside a speech community, variation can still be observed. For example, while it is true that men generally speak differently from women, it is also true that not all women speak alike. These differences can reflect overlapping membership in other static social groupings such as age group, social class, and ethnicity, or they can reflect more dynamic categories such as a speaker's networks of social relations or desire to belong to a particular group or "community of practice." Linguists have described such variations within a speech community as **sociolinguistic discontinuities.**

The recognition of sociolinguistic discontinuities is an important step in trying to understand the **language experience** of Mexican Americans. It allows us to understand the heterogeneous nature of language use in the community and the dynamism that underlies this heterogeneity. If we attempt to describe Mexican American Spanish solely in terms of either regionally bounded speech communities or static social groupings, we find that much of the uniqueness of the language experience is lost. In this chapter, we will pay particular attention to three types of sociolinguistic discontinuities within Mexican American Spanish. First, we will look at proficiency discontinuities that reflect different degrees of exposure to Spanish among Mexican American speakers. Second, we will examine stylistic discontinuities that reflect the restricted contexts in which the minority language is used in U.S. society. Finally, we will consider social discontinuities that reflect the different ways that Mexican American speakers use Spanish in order to establish identity with specific communities of practice.

■ Proficiency Discontinuities

The study of proficiency discontinuities in Mexican American Spanish stems directly from what Benji Wald has called the "boundary problem." According to Wald, the problem "consists of distinguishing the varieties of Mexican American Spanish to be considered as fluent or fully developed from those that are to be considered non-fluent or 'incompletely learned'" (Wald 1989, 57). The boundary problem has been incorporated into research on Mexican American Spanish by proposing a **bilingual continuum** along which speakers continually move throughout their lives.

Carmen Silva-Corvalán's (1994) research on Los Angeles Spanish has set the tone for this type of investigation within Mexican American Spanish. She conceives of the bilingual continuum in terms of an individual's proficiency in each of his or her two languages. The continuum, however, is completely independent of other social variables such as place of birth because a person may move through various locations on the continuum throughout his or her life. This concept yields important insights into the language situation of many Mexican Americans who learn Spanish in the home and English at school. During the preschool years, these individuals would be placed on the Spanish-dominant end of the continuum. After socialization through the Anglo educational system, many Mexican Americans begin to prefer English in all or most contexts, and thus they move closer to the English-dominant end of the continuum.

Silva-Corvalán's work directly accounts for and quantifies movement along the continuum. The central claim of her research is that as speakers move along the continuum toward dominance in one language, the other language tends to recede. It is important to note, however, that minority **language attrition** generally follows an autonomous course that is independent of the dominant language. In other words, as Spanish recedes in the Mexican American community, English language contact may play only an indirect role in the recession. The defining factor in Spanish language attrition is not contact with English, Silva-Corvalán claims, but rather the situation of contact itself. In essence, she argues that many linguistic changes stem from the fact that speakers are burdened with the task of achieving and maintaining communicative competence in two distinct codes at the same time. Speakers lighten the cognitive load through a series of strategies that result in a weakening of the grammatical system of the subordinate language that is in some ways a reversal of language acquisition. Silva-Corvalán observed, "It is arresting to note that some aspects of language loss appear to a certain extent to be the mirror image of development in creolization [a new language formed from the melding of two different languages], and in first and second language acquisition . . . learners go through stages of development which are in some respects the reverse of the stages of loss identified in my data" (Silva-Corvalán 1994, 50).

Absence of the Complementizer *Que*

One example of language recession in the bilingual speech community studied by Silva-Corvalán can be seen in the absence of the complementizer *que* in Los Angeles Spanish discourse. Constructions such as

> I believe that you are wrong
> Yo creo que estás equivocado

are parallel constructions in English and Spanish. In both cases the direct object of the verb is a sentence headed by a complementizer, *que* in Spanish and *that* in English. In English, however, the complement *that* may be omitted, resulting in a construction such as

> I believe you are wrong.

In most varieties of Spanish, on the other hand, the use of *que* is required. It is not possible to formulate a sentence in standard Spanish such as

> Yo creo estás equivocado.

In Los Angeles Spanish, however, Silva-Corvalán found that speakers who were more English dominant tended to extend the complementizer omission rule to Spanish constructions, resulting in expressions such as these:

> Yo creo ⊘ inventaron el nombre. (I think ⊘ they made up the name.)
> Mi mamá no quiere que haga eso. Ella piensa ⊘ si, si no voy full time no voy a terminar. (My mother doesn't want me to do that. She thinks ⊘ if I don't go full time I won't finish.)

These examples support the hypothesis that as speakers move along the bilingual continuum towards greater proficiency in English, they also tend to converge certain rules such as extending the deletion of the complementizer *that* to *que*.

Loss of Aspectual Distinctions

A second example of language attrition along the bilingual continuum can be seen in the use of the two past tense markers in Spanish: the preterite, such as *amé* (loved), and the imperfect, such as *amaba* (used to love). The difference between the preterite and the imperfect reflects an aspectual distinction in Spanish that serves various discursive purposes. For example, to refer to point action in the past, where an event is actualized and completed, speakers would use the preterite tense. To refer to habitual action in the past, where in English we would use the expression *used to,* Spanish speakers would use the imperfect tense. In narrative or storytelling discourse, the imperfect/preterite distinction is used to separate the foregrounded complicating action of the story (that is, the events that happened) from the backgrounded orienting action of the story (the setting and context). The preterite tense is used to move the story along in sequential fashion, indicating that one action occurred immediately after the next. The imperfect tense is used to give background information about other events that were occurring at the same time as the events that make up the story. A simple narrative can illustrate this difference:

> *Había una vez, un niño pescó una rana y se fue pa' su casa feliz porque había pescado una rana y luego le echó a la rana en un frasco.*
> (Once upon a time, a boy caught a frog and he went home happy because he had caught a frog and then he put the frog in a jar; Schecter and Bayley 2002, 119)

In this narrative, we see that the opening backgrounding phrase *Había una vez* (once upon a time) is encoded in the imperfect. The phrases that move the narrative along, however, "caught a frog" (*pescó una rana*), "went home happy" (*se fue pa' su casa feliz*), and "put the frog in a jar" (*le echó a la rana en un frasco*) all appear in the preterite. The phrase "because he had a caught a frog" (*porque había pescado una rana*) occurs in the imperfect because instead of moving the action along, it gives background information about why the boy went home happy.

Silva-Corvalán analyzed this usage among bilingual Mexican American Spanish speakers in Los Angeles. She found that while speakers on the Spanish-dominant end of the bilingual continuum tended to preserve the **semantic** distinction between the preterite and the imperfect in narrative discourse, speakers on the English-dominant end tended to relax the distinction somewhat. For example, one of her informants related a narrative as follows:

> *Y vino y empezamos a pelear, pero ni él ganó ni yo. Y después de eso no había problemas.*
> (And he came and we started fighting, but neither he nor I won. And after that there was never any problem; Silva-Corvalán 1994, 74)

In this example, the phrase "there was never any problem" is part of the complicating action of the story and, thus, would be encoded in the preterite in standard Spanish; however, the speaker encodes the phrase in the imperfect. Silva-Corvalán hypothesizes that this type of relaxation of the semantic difference between the preterite and the imperfect is limited to certain verb types in the Spanish discourse of English-dominant bilingual speakers. She argues that the use of preterite or imperfect verb forms is subordinated to the relative frequency with which some verbs are used. Verbs such as *tener* and *haber* occur frequently in the imperfect. Because of this frequency, speakers tend to **fossilize** the imperfect form and use it even when the preterite is required.

Schecter and Bayley (2002) studied the same variation among Mexican American children in San Antonio. Their findings revealed that children who engaged more frequently in interactions in Spanish in the home tended to be more adept at managing the difference between the imperfect and the preterite while narrating in Spanish. Together, these data suggest that the loss of distinction in the narrative use of preterite and imperfect verb forms directly correlates with the speakers' exposure to Spanish in sustained interactions. As speakers move away from these sustained interactions, the language tends to recede and proficiency discontinuities begin to emerge (see topic highlight 10).

◼ Stylistic Discontinuities

While proficiency discontinuities in Mexican American Spanish show a direct correspondence with the level of proficiency in English and Spanish, stylistic discontinuities reveal a more indirect effect of the influence of English on Spanish. Stylistic discontinuities encompass many features of Mexican American Spanish that deviate from other varieties of Spanish spoken in Mexico and Latin America. The most obvious stylistic discontinuities occur in the ways that certain verb forms are expressed such

Topic Highlight 10. Proficiency Discontinuities in Hypothetical Discourse

Manuel Gutiérrez (1996) studied variation in the verb forms used in future reference conditional ("if-then") sentences in the Spanish spoken by Mexican Americans in Houston. Gutiérrez notes that the conditional construction most common in areas of Mexico such as Michoacán consists of two different verb forms in the condition clause and the result clause. For example, *Si tuviera la oportunidad, regresaría a la escuela.* (If I get the opportunity, I will go back to school.) Gutiérrez's findings reveal that in Houston a new construction is emerging where the verb forms in the condition clause and the result clause are identical. For example, *si tuviera la oportunidad, regresara a la escuela.* Table 4 lists the percentage of utterances in which different and identical verb forms occurred in the data. The data are organized by generation: first generation (respondents born in Mexico), second generation (respondents born in Houston of Mexican-born parents), and third generation (respondents born in Houston of Houston-born parents.

   Analyze these data and determine whether this variation represents a social, a stylistic, or a proficiency discontinuity in Houston Spanish. Explain your answer. ■

Table 4 Verb forms in condition and result clauses of conditional sentences in Houston Spanish.

GENERATION	DIFFERENT VERB FORMS USED (%)	IDENTICAL VERB FORMS USED (%)
First	93	7
Second	56	44
Third	38	62

Data from Gutiérrez 1996.

as *vivemos* instead of *vivimos, traiba* instead of *traía, hablates* instead of *hablaste,* and *vido* instead of *vio.* These stylistic discontinuities are often classified under the general rubric of **archaisms:** forms that were once commonly used in the language but were later replaced by other forms. The persistence of archaisms in the language poses serious questions for the study of Mexican American Spanish. Researchers have generally asked why such forms would persist.

Maryellen García has studied the presence of archaisms and other stylistic discontinuities in Mexican American Spanish. Both the direction and the degree of the discontinuities that she identifies depend crucially on the societal and institutional pressures toward conformity to prescriptive standards (that is, ideas about what is correct speech) rather than on direct or indirect influence from English. One of García's seminal works documented the extension of the preposition *para* to locative phrases where standard varieties use the preposition *a.* In standard Spanish, when the object is concrete, *a* not *para* is used:

Me voy a (not para) San Antonio. (I'm going to San Antonio).

In contrast, when the object is figurative, such as *el Diablo, para* is used:

Vete para el Diablo. (Go to the devil).

Among Mexican American speakers, however, "*para* in locative phrases is losing its semantic feature of indeterminacy and is generalizing in function to indicate the concrete goal of motion, whereas *a* is used to specify goals that can be interpreted either concretely or figuratively" (García 1982, 87). The result of this change is that speakers will say, *Me voy para San Antonio* and *Vete al Diablo* in place of the standard forms.

The social profile of this variable in the border community of El Paso–Ciudad Juárez revealed that the persistence of this stylistic discontinuity will ultimately depend on the pressure to conform to prescriptive usage. While the *para* variant was twice as frequent among El Paso Mexican American speakers as among Juárez Mexican speakers overall, it was nearly as frequent among the *juarense* working class as it was among Mexican Americans in general. Within the Mexican American speakers surveyed, the use of *para* was also most frequent among the working class, but it was quite frequent among the middle class as well. These findings suggest that forms that are characteristic of the working class in Mexican

Spanish become characteristic of working- and middle-class speakers of Mexican American Spanish.

Other studies of stylistic discontinuities in Mexican American Spanish demonstrate a similar pattern. Jaramillo and Bills, for example, examine the variation between the more accepted sound [č] (the first sound in the English word *chip*) and the more stigmatized sound [š] (the first sound in the English word *ship*) in the Spanish of Tomé, New Mexico. (This variation was illustrated in chapter 2 in the alternate pronunciation of the word *boy* as *mushasho* rather than *muchacho*.) Their analysis revealed that speakers more than thirty years of age tended to substitute the [š] sound for the [č] sound almost twice as often as those younger than thirty. They also found that those speakers who had more years of schooling tended to use the [š] sound less, and that those with greater exposure to "formal" Spanish in the New Mexico school system hardly used the sound at all. Their findings "suggest that the use of the [č] variant, especially by younger speakers, is reflective of the operative process of bilingualism. . . . Through education and exposure to standard Spanish, some residents of Tomé may be expanding their command of different varieties of Spanish" (Jaramillo and Bills 1982, 159).

Whereas the locative *para* variant in the Spanish of El Paso is propagating because of the lack of social institutions that promote linguistic norms, the [č] variant in Tomé is becoming more frequent as New Mexican social institutions, specifically the school system, begin to take on the role of promoting standard linguistic norms.

Some language features of Mexican American Spanish appear to overlap as both stylistic and proficiency discontinuities. For example, the variation between the standard pronunciation [b] and the more stigmatized pronunciation [v] was once conceived of as a purely bilingual phenomenon caused by interference from English. Phillips (1975) examined the alternation between [b] and [v] and found that those speakers who claimed to be English dominant produced [v] more frequently. By Phillips' account, this variation would clearly be a case of a proficiency discontinuity. More recently, however, Rena Torres Cacoullos and Fernanda Ferreira (2000) studied the same variation in New Mexican Spanish. They identify two sources for the [v] variant in New Mexico Spanish. Some words contain a "contact [v]," which occurs as a result of the presence of the [v] sound in English. Other words have an "archaic [v]," which is an archaism held over from varieties of Spanish used in colonial times, such as New Mexican

Spanish or Judeo-Spanish. Their examination correlates the presence of the [v] sound with the relative frequency of the words in which it appears. Their findings indicate that archaic [v] is present in high-frequency words and contact [v] is present in low-frequency words. In this case, then, the variation is accounted for on the basis of both a proficiency discontinuity and a stylistic discontinuity.

■ Social Discontinuities

I use the term *social discontinuities* to refer to those unique linguistic practices that correlate with membership in a particular community of practice within the Mexican American community and signal a basic difference from the mainstream society. Social discontinuities emerge as counter-hegemonic discourses that challenge the asymmetrical social relations perceived in the relationship between the Mexican American minority and the European American majority. In this section, we will discuss two examples of this type of sociolinguistic discontinuity. The first example involves what is often referred to as "Chicano caló," the language stereotypically associated with Chicano gang members in the inner-city areas of the Southwest. The second example focuses on "la plática de los viejitos de antes" (the speech of the elders of bygone days) in a northern New Mexico Mexican American community.

Chicano Caló

Chicano caló is often recognized as the characteristic language of criminals in the Southwest. The earliest scientific research on caló seemed to reinforce this stereotype as can be seen in the title of a 1965 study, *The Tongue of the Tirilones: A Linguistic Study of a Criminal Argot*. However, later studies attempted to demystify the criminal aura of caló through systematic investigation of the social contexts in which it was used and the social indices that caló conveyed for its speakers. Linda Fine Katz, in her study of caló in Los Angeles, argued that "for the greatest number of boys . . . the caló was not a criminal argot, but rather a language which conveyed their practical needs and interests and which as a result, they enjoyed using" (Katz 1974, 40). In trying to show the differences between insider and outsider perceptions of caló, Katz goes on to note that "more than anger or hatred, my informants spoke of pride—pride in creating and using a language which allowed them to 'show how sharp we were and which made us feel as if we understood each other'" (p. 41). Rosaura Sánchez further elucidates this in-group view of caló as a manifestation of cultural pride and solidarity. "Caló then is a highly creative code which utilizes a number of techniques to produce an effect of authenticity. . . . Caló is not a secret language. As an intra-group sub-code, it is an element in group solidarity" (Sánchez 1994, 134). As an in-group, solidarity-forming code, Chicano caló reveals several characteristics that highlight verbal creativity and that directly reflect the "sharpness" of its users.

Chicano caló consists largely of innovative vocabulary items, although prosodic (rhythm and intonation) features play an important role in its successful deployment. Innovative vocabulary derives from both English and Spanish sources, and the new words often reflect the arbitrariness of the sound-meaning relationship. One characteristic trait of Chicano caló is what Rosaura Sánchez has called **over-coding.** Over-coding occurs when a word is assigned a different meaning based on its syntactic (word order) positioning and its phonetic similarity (similarity in sound) with another word. For example, Chicano caló speakers can respond in the affirmative by saying *simon* instead of *sí*. Other examples include

Ay nos vidrios = Ahí nos vemos (See you later.)
Es para miguelito = Es para mí (It's for me.)
Ya estufas = Ya estuvo (That's it.)

In the examples here, the semantic over-coding depends solely on the phonetic similarities that exist between two unrelated Spanish words. Other examples of over-coding depend on the phonetic similarities that exist between two unrelated words in different languages. Words such as *birria* 'beer' and *refinar* 'to eat' exemplify this process. The word *birria* refers to a shredded beef dish in many parts of Mexico, but it takes on a new meaning in caló due to its phonetic similarity with the English word *beer*. The word *refinar* in standard Spanish means 'to refine' or 'to purify'; however, because of its phonetic similarity with the English word *refill*, it has taken on the meaning of 'to eat'. The process of over-coding can also be entirely semantic (meaning-based). In words such as *pinto* 'prisoner' and *borlo* 'dance', the over-coding process results from an extension and focusing of an existing word in the language. The word *pinto* typically means 'spotted'. In caló, the meaning of *pinto* is extended to include the meaning of 'striped' and thus was semantically focused to refer to prisoners who wear striped uniforms. The word *borlote* means 'uproar'. The word was

■ 7. The EZ-Loan pawn shop in Alton, Texas, announces that it accepts payments on bills, or "biles," from major utility companies. (Photograph by Glenn Martínez)

semantically focused to refer to a dance and then phonetically shortened to become *borlo*. The use of these over-coded words gives caló speakers access to a possibly infinite number of new phrases that both tie them together in bonds of solidarity and set them apart as *más truchas* (very smart).

Other innovative words stem from English and reflect the unique social context of caló speakers. The term **borrowing** is often used to refer to words taken from one language and adapted to fit the sound system of another. Many borrowings have been generalized in Mexican American Spanish and are not specifically associated with caló. A pawn shop sign in Alton, Texas, announces that it accepts bills, or *"biles,"* from major utility companies (see figure 7). Borrowings associated with caló are *huachear* 'to watch' or 'to see', *clica* 'clique' or 'gang', *jainita* 'honey' or 'girl', and *waifa* 'wife'. Chicano caló speakers also assign new meanings to existing Spanish words. The term **calque** is often used to describe this process. Chicano caló calques include words such as *tubo* (tube) 'television', *tanque* (tank) 'prison', and *rata* (rat) 'informant'.

While Chicano caló opens up a space for solidarity building among Mexican Americans in inner-city barrios, it also directly confronts and subverts the dominant spaces of mainstream America. This may be one of the primary reasons why it has been stereotyped as a criminal, non-mainstream, against-the-grain linguistic practice. As Raúl Homero Villa argues "barrio residents have consciously and unconsciously enacted resistive tactics or defensive mechanisms to secure and preserve the integrity of their cultural place identity within and against the often hostile space regulation of dominant urbanism" (Villa 2000, 5). Chicano caló is a counter-hegemonic discourse that uses verbal behavior to mark out specific spaces as belonging to Chicanos.

La Plática de los Viejitos de Antes

Counter-hegemonic discourses can also be observed in rural Mexican American communities. Charles Briggs (1988), for example, studied a particular way of talking characteristic of the elders of northern New Mexico that he calls "la plática de los viejitos de antes." This type of discourse consists of the use of various **genres**—proverbs, scriptural allusions, historical discourse, legends, hymns, and prayers—in order to convey an essential meaning from the *antes* 'bygone days' that is relevant to the *ahora* 'here and now'. In the following extract, we can see some of the features of la plática at work.

> *Todos corrían tras de ellas*
> *Ah, pero pa' cuidarlas, sanamabí*
> *como andaban, andaba uno con teguas ¿no?*
> (Everybody used to run after them
> Oh, but taking care of them, son-of-a-bitch
> the way they wandered, we were wearing moccasins, right?; Briggs 1988, 68–69)

First, la plática de los viejitos de antes is multifunctional. This means that within la plática a single linguistic form can signal more than one function. The word *teguas* 'moccasins' in this example serves the function of referring to an object. The choice of the regional colonial Spanish term *teguas* instead of the more standard *mocasinas,* however, also serves a more general or encyclopedic function marking a difference between bygone days and the here and now. The use of the word *teguas* also serves an indexical function by drawing participants into bygone days and expanding the frame of reference of the hearer. When the speaker uses the word teguas, the hearer is immediately shifted to a different time. Briggs explains that teguas

> point, on the one hand, to the poverty of the people in bygone days. Teguas were produced in the community because Córdovans were too poor to afford shoes. The elders generally describe moccasins in derogatory terms, noting that they absorbed moisture from the rain or snow and then stiffened as they dried. Moccasins evoke, on the other hand, the way that elders of bygone days compensated for their poverty through hard work and resourcefulness. (p. 77)

A second feature of la plática that can be observed in this example is **dialogism.** This means that "the performance is shaped in keeping with an ongoing exchange between participants" (Briggs 1988, 354). In the example, we see that while the speaker conveys referential, encyclopedic, and indexical functions of antes through the use of the word *teguas,* he also conveys similar functions of ahora with the use of the borrowed word *sanamabí.* This word contextualizes the discourse within the present, even while the following line recontextualizes the discourse within the past.

Briggs' observations of this kind of talk in northern New Mexico suggested that not every member of the speech community was equally adept in rendering this type of speech. In fact, he found that even members who knew the words of specific proverbs or legends, for example, claimed an inability to engage in this type of discourse. Members of the *mexicano* speech community reserved a special place for those speakers who could successfully engage in la plática de los viejitos de antes in just the right context in order to make a point about the current state of affairs within their community. These speakers were believed to possess *el don* (the gift) that allowed them to *traer sentido* (give meaning) to language practices. La plática de los viejitos de antes, therefore, consists of the deployment of particular language features in appropriate social settings in order to convey a basic meaning about social relationships in the here and now. While la plática de los viejitos de antes consists of a variety of genres of talk, Briggs was able to uncover several characteristics that underlie the successful use of *el don.*

Through its constitutive traits of multifunctionality and dialogism, la plática de los viejitos de antes serves as a counter-hegemonic discourse that at once challenges the social asymmetries between the in-group and the out-group and within the in-group as well. Briggs explains,

> performers do not focus simply on the way that others, Mexicanos or Americanos, have internalized the dominant hegemony—the performers also point their fingers at themselves and their communities. Much more attention is devoted in the talk of elders of bygone days to Mexicanos who have aligned themselves in one way or another with the dominant hegemony than to Anglo-Americans. (Briggs 1988, 368)

As such, this discourse serves as a means for the community to contest social inequality and the forms of domination that exist as well as to retain and reclaim a place identity.

Concluding Thoughts

In this chapter, we have discussed Mexican American Spanishes by concentrating on the two-way relationship between social and linguistic variation. While all languages vary, they vary in different ways, both across speech communities and within speech communities. The social patterns that characterize the Mexican American experience lead to unique patterns of sociolinguistic discontinuities that affect and are affected by the lived experiences of Mexican Americans in the Southwest. Proficiency discontinuities represent a direct linguistic manifestation of the processes of **language shift** discussed in chapter 3. As speakers move further away from sustained and continual usage of the language, the language system can begin to recede. Stylistic discontinuities reflect the role of social institutions in the language that is used by the speech community. We saw that in some cases, certain nonstandard language forms were being propagated because of the lack of language-normalizing institutions. We also saw other cases where a standard language form was beginning to take the place of a regional nonstandard form, a change directly correlated with the increasing presence of formal Spanish instruction in the schools. Finally, we looked at social discontinuities, those language forms that set apart a particular community of practice within the Mexican American community and that serve as a counter-hegemonic discourse to signal the social asymmetries present in the wider society.

■ Discussion Exercises

1. What is the bilingual continuum?

2. What relationship exists between language variation and social institutions such as schools, the media, and churches?

3. Explain the concept of semantic over-coding and give examples from Chicano caló.

4. What is the difference between borrowing and calquing?

5. Explain the multifunctionality of la plática de los viejitos de antes.

6. How does Chicano caló converge with la plática de los viejitos de antes in forming a unified counter-hegemonic discourse that challenges social inequality and domination both within and outside the Mexican American speech community?

7. Analyze the following discourse of Aurelio Trujillo, a *viejito* (elder) from Córdova, New Mexico. Discuss how multifunctionality and dialogism are apparent in this plática.

> Pero al cabo que, al cabo que Dios los, los sabe premiar, lo mismo que premia al pecador, porque dice "perdonad al inocente," dice, "porque no sabe lo que hace." Y todos semos hijos, todos semos brothers, todos semos hermanos. Y muchos no, porque tiene un nickel more que el otro; es orgullo. Mire, la vanidad se acaba, no tiene fin. El dinero se acaba, no tiene fin. De modo que hay tres cosas que no tienen fin. Y la, y la amistad reina en la vida. (Briggs 1988, 146)
>
> (But because, because God knows how to reward them. Just as he rewards the sinner because he says "forgive the innocent," he says, "because they don't know what they do." And we are all children, we are all brothers. But many are not because they have a nickel more than someone else; it's pride. Look, vanity is never ending, it is pointless. Money is never ending, it is pointless. In the same way, there are three things that are pointless. And, and friendship reigns supreme in life.)

■ Suggested Readings

Bowen, J. Donald, and Jacob Ornstein eds. *Studies in Southwest Spanish*. Rowley, MA: Newbury House, 1976.

Briggs, Charles L. *Competence in Performance: The Creativity of Tradition in Mexicano Verbal Art*. Philadelphia: University of Pennsylvania Press, 1988.

Silva-Corvalán, Carmen. *Language Contact and Change: Spanish in Los Angeles*. New York: Oxford University Press, 1994.

5

Mexican American English

O ne of the initial debates in the study of Mexican American English revolved around the question of whether it should be considered a native variety of English or a Spanish-influenced transitional language that would eventually converge on one of the regional dialects of English. Some researchers have viewed Mexican American English as nothing more than English with a Spanish accent. In her study of bilingualism in San Antonio, for example, Janet Sawyer stated that "the English spoken by the bilingual informants was simply an imperfect state in the mastery of English . . . in the community under study for this report, there was no Mexican American English dialect" (Sawyer 1975, 78). In contrast, other scholars recognize Mexican American English as a set of stable features, sometimes arising from Spanish influence, that is shared among large numbers of Mexican American speakers. Allan Metcalf, for example, defined Chicano English as "a variety of English that is obviously influenced by Spanish and that has low prestige in most circles, but that nevertheless is independent of Spanish and is the first, and often only, language of many hundreds of thousands of residents of California" (Metcalf 1974, 53).

The early scholarly discussions on the status of Mexican American English severely misconceived the defining characteristics of a native variety of a language. Nativization of a language is not a question of the presence or absence of a set of measurable linguistic features, it is more a question of the multiple ways in which individual speakers use the language to meet their communicative needs (see topic highlight 11). In the **language experience** of Mexican Americans, English is not necessarily a strictly homogenizing and acculturating agent. On the contrary, the presence of English in Mexican American communities oftentimes responds to unique code repertoires (Kachru 1986) in which the functions of English coexist with equally important functions in Spanish. Otto Santa Ana, for instance, suggests,

Topic Highlight 11. Nativizing English, Chicano Style

In his novel *Pocho*, José Antonio Villareal writes,

> Mary stood speechless with wonder as Richard and his mother spoke to each other in Spanish. "She talks funny," she said. "We all do. That's the Spanish.... A long time ago, the Spanish was the only way I could talk. Then I went to school and they taught me to talk like this. I've been trying to teach my father and mother to talk English, but I don't think they really want to learn." (Villareal 1959, 133)

The words of José Antonio Villareal's young protagonist, Richard Rubio, unveil the problem of defining Chicano English from a unique perspective. In looking at the way Richard Rubio uses English, we see obvious Spanish influences. For instance, instead of saying, "That's Spanish," Rubio exclaims, "That's the Spanish." The use of the definite article before the name of a language is obviously a case of transfer from Spanish where the construction *el español* would be the norm. However, despite the Spanish influence in Rubio's English, it is all the same his English—so much so that he wants to teach it to his parents as well. ■

The **language shift** of the Chicanos from a predominantly Spanish-speaking to a predominantly English-speaking community since 1945 may well have been accompanied by a shift of the cultural value of their English dialect. In this latter view it could be argued that the markers of ethnicity and acculturation are to be found in Chicano English, rather than in the maintenance of Southwest Spanish. Indeed, there is solid evidence that Chicano culture is maintained in spite of the loss of Spanish among younger Chicanos. (Santa Ana 1993, 12)

The study of Mexican American English, then, should focus not so much on the question of how much Spanish influence is present or where that influence might be seen, but rather on how the language coexists within a unique ecology that sustains a plurality of languages.

In our study of Mexican American English, we will look specifically at the ways that English thrives in the Mexican American community. In particular, we will analyze some of the linguistic features that point to the growing importance and continuing vitality of English in the Mexican American language experience. The discussion of these linguistic features will bear out the multidimensionality of Mexican American English by pointing to the complex and intersecting influences of regional English, African American English, and Spanish on the dialect. First, we will look at transfer phenomena from Spanish and discuss the ways in which Spanish-influenced English has been nativized in the Mexican American community. Second, we will look at the influence of other dialects of English and discuss the ways that Mexican American English converges on other minority dialects of English in the United States. Finally, we will look at the pronunciation of Spanish onomastics—that is, names of people and places—in Mexican American English and discuss some of the reasons why Spanish **phonology** persists in these words.

■ Vernacularization in Mexican American English

The difficulties surrounding the definition of Mexican American English are couched in the high degrees of heterogeneity found in the speech communities in which Mexican Americans participate. Walking into a grocery store in any one of the numerous Mexican American barrios in the Southwest, the casual observer is faced with an astounding degree of linguistic heterogeneity. Over the intercom, the grocery manager might be announcing the daily specials in what could be considered standard northern Mexican Spanish. A father scolds his child in a more popular variety of Spanish. A cashier requests a price check in a regional dialect of English, and so on. Mexican American English is one strand of this colorful linguistic tapestry that characterizes the Mexican American community. Mexican American English thus coexists with both a variety of Spanishes and a variety of Englishes.

According to Santa Ana (1993, 23), "Vernacular Chicano English is defined as the dialect of Chicano speakers of English who have minimum contact with non-Chicanos in their daily communicative life." The degree of contact with non-Chicanos, however, varies considerably according to the specific lived experiences of the speakers. Thus, Mexican American English, instead of being viewed as a unified language variety with little space for variation, might be more adequately described in terms of a continuum. Leticia Galindo points out that "on a linguistic continuum, we could possibly find a variety [of English] that purports to be a standard form of Chicano English; on the other end of this continuum, we could find a non-standard variety arising out of language contact with other non-standard varieties of English such as vernacular Black English" (Galindo 1987, 4). Returning to the metaphor of the tapestry, then, we might conceive of Mexican American English as a strand of changing hues that seamlessly blends into the colorful scene.

The most salient linguistic features of Mexican American English are often regarded as transfer features from Spanish. Fromkin and Rodman, in their introductory text on linguistics, for instance, state that "Chicano English is, like other dialects, the result of many factors, a major one being the influence of Spanish" (Fromkin and Rodman 1988, 269–70). They support this contention by pointing out a number of phonological features of Mexican American English, including the non-differentiation of the tense and lax articulations of the [i] vowel sound. The vowel sound in *ship* is lax (in English class you called it a short vowel sound), and the vowel sound in *sheep* is tense (a long vowel). Many Mexican American English speakers pronounce these two words exactly the same. Other features include the alternation of [č] (the "ch" sound in *chip*) and [š] (the "sh" sound in *ship*) sounds so that *show* often sounds like *cho* and the word *check* often sounds like *sheck*. These features have been studied extensively in the literature with surprising results. While we would assume that these accented English features would fade away after several generations, researchers have found that many Spanish-influenced features in English phonology persist well into the fourth and fifth generations.

For example, Otto Santa Ana (1991) studied the variation of vowel sounds in the English spoken in East Los Angeles by four generations of Mexican Americans. His findings revealed that the same pattern found among first-generation speakers persisted among fourth-generation speakers. However, he noted that the persistence of the pattern depended largely on the degree of social achievement outside of the barrio. Fourth-generation speakers who were upwardly mobile and who had a variety of contacts outside of East LA tended to move away from the Spanish-influenced pronunciation while those with relatively few contacts outside of the barrio tended to retain it.

Galindo (1987) conducted a study of tense [i] (as in *sheep*) and lax [I] (as in *ship*) in the English of Mexican Americans in Austin, Texas. She conducted **sociolinguistic interviews** with thirty Mexican American adolescents from the Austin area. The sample was equally divided between males and females and bilingual and English-dominant speakers. The interviews dealt with a variety of topics. Female interviewees often discussed *quinceañeras* while male interviewees preferred to talk about sports and social activities. Each interview lasted from forty-five to sixty minutes.

After transcribing the interviews, Galindo counted the total number of words that would be pronounced in standard English with lax [I] sounds and determined the number of these pronounced with a tense vowel and with a lax vowel. Of a total of 2,779 realizations of the /I/ sound, 340 were pronounced as tense [i]. Most speakers tended to produce the tense [i] when the following sound was either an [n]—so the word *sin* might sound more like *seen*—or an [l]—so the word *fill* might sound more like *feel*. After tabulating the data in this way, Galindo set out to see whether factors such as bilingualism and sex had any relevant effect on pronunciation. Her analysis revealed that bilingualism was a crucial factor in the pronunciation of tense [i]. Bilingual speakers were nearly twice as likely as English-dominant speakers to use tense [i] instead of lax [I]. At the same time, however, female speakers were more likely than male speakers to use the tense [i]. Galindo offers the following explanation:

> Females seem to be linguistically secure in that they may not feel a sense of shame or inferiority to admit they speak Spanish. In addition, they are under less pressure to conform to other linguistic norms as a sign of in-group identity or social acceptance. Most of these females come from traditional homes whereby males are allowed ample freedom to come and go as they please compared to females. (Galindo 1987, 118)

Galindo's findings demonstrate that even while Spanish-influenced features of Mexican American English correlate highly with bilingualism, they also correlate with other social variables that exist in the speech community. The more frequent pronunciation of tense [i] among Mexican American females in the Austin speech community suggests that this particular linguistic feature is beginning to stand out not just as a marker of Spanish-influenced English, but also as a marker of gender identity in the community.

Both the Santa Ana and Galindo studies suggest that Spanish-influenced linguistic features are, through a process of nativization, becoming part of the Mexican American dialect of English. This process of nativization involves the systematic reconstitution of the social meaning of linguistic variables. Whereas the pronunciation of *fit* as *feet* might signal imperfect or accented English in an Anglo speech community, this pronunciation is supplanted by different meanings in the Mexican American community. These processes of reconstitution are an essential facet of Mexican American English.

Janina Brutt-Griffler proposes the concept of macroacquisition to explain this type of reconstitution. When an individual takes on the task of learning a second language, he or she will normally seek to become immersed in a speech community that uses the second language. This type of language learning could be called microacquisition because it involves a single individual entering into a much larger speech community. Macroacquisition, on the other hand, is "the process of second language acquisition by speech communities" (Brutt-Griffler 2002, 11). Macroacquisition is thus an entire speech community adapting to and acquiring a new language. It is, in essence, another way of looking at the process of language shift discussed in chapter 3.

When a speech community relinquishes one language in favor of another over the course of several generations, it does not necessarily relinquish its unique identity and become absorbed by existing speech communities. Instead, a process of **vernacularization** may occur, in which a language undergoing macroacquisition comes into primary usage. "This process transforms the bilingual community into a primarily monolingual community using what was originally the second language. Vernacularization thus involves language shift with concomitant language change—the development of a new variety" (Brutt-Griffler 2002, 169). While the Mexican American community has clearly not shifted entirely to English, major sections of it have shifted either partially or totally in that direction. Together with this shift—partial or total—we are witnessing a process of vernacularization in which Mexican American English is becoming a unique social dialect that expresses and indexes the complex language experience of the Mexican American community.

■ Minority Dialect Convergence in Mexican American English

Vernacularization is an important contributing factor in the development of Mexican American English; however, it is not the only factor to influence its development. Other factors, such as contact with other nonstandard varieties of English, also play a key role in the emergence of Mexican American English.

African American Vernacular English (AAVE) is an important source of many of the features of Mexican American English. Galindo (1987) studied the presence of AAVE features in the English of her Austin sample. She found that AAVE features such as the pronunciation *fightin'* instead of *fighting* were most common among male adolescents.

Carmen Fought (2003) carried out similar studies among Mexican Americans in southern California. In her study, she focused on the well-known AAVE feature referred to as *negative concord.* Negative concord is the use of a double negative in a sentence. The most common types of negative concord include the use of a negative auxiliary and an adverb, as in *I won't do it no more,* and the use of a negative auxiliary and a pronoun, as in *I can't say nothing.* These highly stigmatized constructions occur frequently in AAVE (Labov 1972).

Fought set out to study the use of negative concord among thirty-six southern California Mexican Americans between the ages of fifteen and thirty-five. She conducted sociolinguistic interviews with each participant and analyzed the correlation between negative concord and the following social factors: sex, social class, and gang affiliation. The gang affiliation variable covered a wide range of possibilities. "Gang members" were individuals who were members of a bona fide Los Angeles gang; "gang affiliates" were those who knew someone who was a member of a bona fide Los Angeles gang; "non-gang members" were neither members nor affiliates of a gang; and "taggers" were those who made a concerted effort to be perceived as gang members even though they had no actual connection to a gang. Fought's analysis revealed no significant correlation with gender. The other two social variables correlated positively with the use of negative concord. For instance, low-income speakers used negative concord almost twice as often as middle-class speakers. Similarly, individuals with a real or imagined gang affiliation used negative concord with much higher frequencies than those who claimed to have no gang affiliation at all. The degree of involvement in gangs, moreover, directly correlated with the use of negative concord (see table 5).

This pattern of variation reveals that negative concord is a salient marker of gang identity within the Mexican American community. Interestingly, the taggers, those with a contrived gang affiliation, made the most frequent use of negative concord. Fought comments that "the taggers seem

Table 5 Use of negative concord by gang affiliation

GANG INVOLVEMENT	NEGATIVE CONCORD (%)
Tagger	69
Gang member	56
Gang affiliate	41
Non-gang member	19

Data from Fought 2003.

to be trying to talk more 'tough' than even the gangsters, by using even more negative concord" (Fought 2003, 150).

These data suggest that Mexican American English is influenced not only by its Spanish substrate and by the processes of vernacularization that co-occur with varied processes of language shift, but also by the minority status of its speakers in the U.S. context. Galindo seems to dismiss this possibility, stating,

> Chicanos and Blacks share similar features within their respective varieties of English; however, they may have been acquired through different sources, including but not confined to Spanish. Those features initially perceived as being unique to Vernacular Black English emerged in other nonstandard varieties of American and British English. Therefore, we can conclude that description of variable phenomena must not be viewed in terms of a single linguistic source but accept the fact that variation is oftentimes the result of a convergence of sources. (Galindo 1987, 182)

Fought's data, however, suggest a quite different interpretation. Given the fact that the variation occurs most significantly within the social space where AAVE and Mexican American English converge, namely, in gang subculture, it would seem that there is a very direct relation between the use of linguistic features such as negative concord in the two dialects.

Regional Dialect Convergence in Mexican American English

In the same way that Mexican American English tends to adopt features of AAVE, it has also been shown to adopt features of the regional varieties of

English spoken in the matrix society. Mexican American English in California, for example, may differ in certain features from Mexican American English in Texas. In her southern California study, Carmen Fought (2003) encountered several features of Mexican American English that converge on regional California English. Specifically, she found a high occurrence of the quotative discourse markers *be like* and *be all*. These discourse markers are used to signal quotations in a stream of discourse. Some examples of quotative *be like* include

> She's like "no, you leave the house when you get married."
> I was like "don't worry about it, man." (Fought 2003, 108)

The *be all* discourse marker has a similar function, as seen in these examples:

> He's all, you know, "what's your name?"
> I was all "am I going to be alright?" (p. 108)

Fought points out that "the use of . . . quotatives associated with California . . . reinforces this picture of Chicano English in Los Angeles as a *Californian* dialect of English" (p. 109).

Roger Thompson conducted a study of a regional phonological (pronunciation) variable among forty Mexican Americans raised in Austin, Texas. His study bears out the Texas regional influence on Mexican American English. He studied the process of vowel fronting in words like *five, dime,* and *hide* where the low back vowel in the diphthong is fronted. This results in the southern "twang" where these words sound like "fahve," "dahme," and "hahde." This feature of regional Texas English is so salient that Thompson (1975, 20) argues "if Mexican Americans are consciously patterning their speech after a regional model, this feature would probably be one of the first [features] to be adopted." In his analysis of vowel fronting in Mexican American English in Texas, Thompson compared three social correlates with Mexican Americans' use of the regional features of Texas English: (1) the language used at work, (2) highest grade of schooling completed, and (3) socioeconomic status. The results of his study indicated that among Mexican Americans who used Spanish at work, fifteen out of twenty speakers used the non-regional pronunciation. Among those who used English at work, however, ten speakers used the regional pronunciation and the other ten used the non-regional pronunciation (see table 6). In terms of the level of schooling achieved by the speakers, Thompson found

Table 6 Social correlates with use of Texas regional pronunciation

SOCIAL FACTOR	NON-REGIONAL PRONUNCIATION	REGIONAL PRONUNCIATION
Language used at work		
Spanish	15	5
English	10	10
Highest grade of school completed		
0–9th grade	18	4
10th grade or higher	7	11
Socioeconomic status		
Upper	16	4
Lower	9	11

Data from Thompson 1975.

that the more educated speakers tended to favor the regional pronunciation while those with the least amount of education overwhelmingly preferred the non-regional pronunciation. Finally, with respect to socioeconomic status, Thompson's data showed that speakers with lower socioeconomic status preferred the non-regional pronunciation while those with higher socioeconomic status slightly preferred the regional pronunciation. These data attest to the fact that regional pronunciation of English among Mexican Americans in Texas is associated with upward social mobility and success (Thompson 1975, 18–24).

These studies show that the sources of Mexican American English encompass a wide variety of possibilities including the matrix dialect itself. Otto Santa Ana argues that "rather than a regionally unique collage of unrelated linguistic varieties, the language and dialect contact situation of Chicanos can best be considered as a coherent phenomenon, encompassing regional variation, monolingualism in two languages, and shades of bilingualism. The basis of its unity is the commonality of Chicano ethnicity" (Santa Ana 1993, 22).

Acts of Identity in Mexican American English

A final feature of Mexican American English that deserves attention is the unique pronunciation of onomastics. Mexican Americans oftentimes pronounce names of places, food, and people preserving the Spanish pronun-

Table 7 Onomastic pronunciations by generation in a Texas Mexican American family

GENERATION	SPANISH PHONOLOGY (%)	ENGLISH PHONOLOGY (%)
Grandparents	65	35
Parents	37	63
Children	38	62

Data from Doran 2001.

ciation even though they have no intention of switching to Spanish. Mexican American English speakers often pronounce Spanish place-names such as San Antonio, El Paso, Juárez, and Reynosa; food names such as fajitas, enchiladas, and chorizo; and names of people such as José, Juan, and María using Spanish phonology. This practice, sometimes viewed as annoyingly "ethnic" by mainstream monolingual English speakers, is a mechanism that allows Mexican American English speakers to assert their ethnic identity even when the language they are speaking obscures it. At the same time, the use of English phonology to render Spanish-origin names is often looked down upon in Mexican American discourse. The rendering of Univisión as [yunəvižən] ("Yunivishn") or *fajitas* as [fəhifəz] ("fuhidus") often comes off as snobbish and an implicit betrayal of one's heritage.

Amanda Doran (2001) studied this linguistic phenomenon in the Texas border city of El Paso. In this study, Doran observed eight members of a middle-class, English-dominant Mexican American family in El Paso. The members of the family comprised three generations including grandparents, parents, and children. Doran studied 13.5 hours of informal conversations involving these family members and supplemented her findings with participant-observation. Doran counted all of the Spanish-origin names in the conversations and determined the distribution of English and Spanish pronunciations. Her findings revealed that the grandparents used Spanish phonology more consistently than the parents or the children. At the same time, however, the parents and the children used Spanish phonology with about the same frequency (see table 7).

Given the fact that although the children claimed to be much more comfortable speaking in English than in Spanish, it is surprising that they used Spanish phonology as often as their parents did. Doran's analysis of the speech of two disc jockeys at an El Paso Top 40 radio station, however, sheds some light on this pattern. Whereas in the family domain, Doran studied informal conversation, with the disc jockeys she studied the speech used in on-air announcements. Doran describes the differences in some detail:

> There are many differences between informal conversational speech and the speech of radio announcers. For example, radio speech tends to be more planned, or rehearsed (if only through practice), than informal conversational speech, though much effort is made to make it sound spontaneous. In addition, the content of radio speech is more limited, it often contains frequent repetition of information, it is often directed towards an absent audience, and the errors that occur in the course of radio speech tend to be much more noticeable. (Doran 2001, 52)

The contrast between these two types of speech enabled Doran to discern more clearly the community-wide norms among Mexican Americans in El Paso. The analysis of Spanish onomastics among the disc jockeys revealed that Spanish-origin names were pronounced with Spanish phonology 31 percent of the time. This is quite similar to the speech of both the parents and the children in the informal conversational data. The symmetry between the speech of the parents, the children, and the disc jockeys suggests that there may be a certain degree of conventionalization among Mexican American English speakers with respect to the pronunciation of Spanish names. Doran found that personal names were more likely to be pronounced with Spanish phonology than were place-names. Within the category of place-names, furthermore, she found that names on the Mexican side of the border, such as Ciudad Juárez and Chihuahua, were more likely to be pronounced with Spanish phonology than names on the U.S. side of the border. For example, the place-name El Paso was normally rendered with English phonology. One family member commented that "certain words, like Juárez, only sound right when pronounced with Spanish phonology while others, like El Paso, only sound right when pronounced with English phonology" (Doran 2001, 167). Food names, on the other hand, were normally pronounced with Spanish phonology in the informal conversational data but they were pronounced with English phonology in the more formal speech of disc jockeys.

Doran sums up her study by stating, "One of my most important findings pertains to the English spoken by the youngest generation of family members and the disc jockeys. I found that even these speakers, whose English is in most respects indistinguishable from non–Mexican American speakers of 'standard' and other local varieties of English, distinguished themselves linguistically from non–Mexican Americans" (Doran 2001, 258). Such acts of identity are routinely seen and heard throughout the Southwest. Doran's study strikes at an extremely important source for Mexican American English. While vernacularization and minority status certainly play roles in the formation of Mexican American dialects of English, the most important factor is that of identity. The use of linguistic resources in order to express a unique, socially and historically grounded, ethnic identity can occur both consciously and unconsciously, and it can occur through numerous mechanisms, including vernacularization, convergence with other nonstandard dialects, use of Spanish phonology, and as we will see in the following chapter, **code switching.**

■ Concluding Thoughts

In this chapter we have considered Mexican American English from a variety of perspectives. We have confronted the complexity of the dialect by recognizing its great variety of sources. We found that many features of Mexican American English do, in fact, arise from the Spanish language substrate of the dialect. For example, the convergence of tense [i] and lax [I] in the English of Mexican Americans in Texas makes words like *fill* and *feel* and *pill* and *peal* homophonous. This pronunciation, typical of a learner of English as a second language, is also becoming common among English-dominant speakers in the Mexican American community and is thus acquiring new social meanings in the speech community. Because of this, the presence of these Spanish substrate features may reflect a process of vernacularization that is turning these features into native dialect features.

We also saw that other features of Mexican American English emerge from linguistic convergence with other minority dialects such as AAVE. For example, negative concord has become a symbol of gang affiliation in the Mexican American English of southern California. In the same vein, we saw that majority regional dialects also contribute to Mexican American English. In Mexican American English in California, for example, we found a rather frequent occurrence of quotative discourse markers such as *be like* and *be all,* and in Mexican American English in Texas, we found that phonological features associated with a southern twang were associated with upward social mobility and success. Finally, we looked at the pronunciation of Spanish onomastics in Mexican American English and found a pattern in the English of El Paso where certain lexical items were normally pronounced with Spanish phonology regardless of the speaker's ability to use that language in a communicative setting. While Mexican American English is a complex phenomenon that resists any single and straightforward definition, it is fundamentally the ability of Mexican Americans to seize linguistic resources in order to express a common ethnic identity.

■ Discussion Exercises

1. What is macroacquisition? How does it differ from microacquisition?

2. Why would a native speaker of English use certain language features that are characteristic of nonnative speakers?

3. Why did taggers use negative concord more often than any other group in Carmen Fought's study?

4. What kinds of regional dialect features emerge in the Mexican American English of southern California? What kinds of features emerge in the Mexican American English of Texas?

5. What patterns emerge in the use of Spanish phonology to pronounce Spanish onomastics in El Paso English?

6. In her book *Chicano English in Context,* Carmen Fought introduces four myths about Mexican American English. Consider each one and formulate an argument as to why you think it is a myth.

    Myth 1: Chicano English is spoken by people whose first language is Spanish, and interference from Spanish introduces mistakes in their English.

    Myth 2: Chicano English is the same thing as "Spanglish."

    Myth 3: Chicano English is a dialect spoken mostly by gang members, not by middle-class Latinos/as.

    Myth 4: Chicano English is merely incorrect grammar. (Fought 2003, 3–8)

7. Consider the following scene from José Antonio Villareal's novel *Pocho*. What is Richard Rubio trying to get across to his father? Why does Juan Rubio vehemently reject his son's argument? Is there an intermediary option? How does the emergence of Mexican American English embody that option?

"Silence!" roared Juan Rubio. "We will not speak the dog language in my house!" They were at the supper table.

"But this is America, Father," said Richard. "If we live in this country, we must live like Americans."

"And next you will tell me that those are not tortillas you are eating but bread, and those are not beans but *hahm an'ecks*."

"No, but I mean that you must remember that we are not in Mexico. In Mexico. . . ."

"*Hahm an'ecks*," his father interrupted. (Villareal 1959, 133)

■ Suggested Readings

Fought, Carmen. *Chicano English in Context*. New York: Palgrave, 2003.

Ornstein-Galicia, Jacob, ed. *Form and Function in Chicano English*. Malabar, FL: Robert Krieger Publishing, 1988.

Penfield, Joyce, and Jacob Ornstein-Galicia. *Chicano English: An Ethnic Contact Dialect*. Amsterdam: John Benjamins, 1985.

6

Mexican American Code Switching

As we have seen in the previous two chapters, the language of the Mexican American minority presents unique characteristics in both Spanish and English. The most salient characteristic of Mexican American speech, however, is not to be found in either Spanish or English, but rather in the sustained usage of both languages in a single sentence or discourse event. Scholars refer to this linguistic practice as **code switching.**

While code switching may appear odd to many monolingual speakers, it is reflective of the type of linguistic practice used in every single speech community in the world. In monolingual speech communities, the pattern of code switching is reflected in the linguistic dexterity of speakers who switch from one accent or speech variety to another with the intention of producing a certain effect. For example, a storyteller may bring a story to life by switching from a New York accent to a southern accent and back again. Public speakers often switch from a formal speech pattern to a more informal one when making a joke in order to convey the relatively less serious tone of that particular segment of their presentation.

In bilingual communities, the potential for this type of linguistic dexterity is multiplied several times over. Bilingual speakers may choose to switch between languages or between varieties and styles within each language. This linguistic dexterity, however, is often misunderstood and at times even maligned. Many speakers tend to view code switching as a sort of watered down language that reflects an inability to use either language for sustained periods of time. This erroneous view fails to consider the social effects that bilingual speakers achieve when they switch from one language to another. In the same way that a monolingual English speaker purposefully switches from one variety or style within English to carry out a specific social function, the bilingual speaker also chooses to use both languages in unique constellations in order to make a specific point or achieve a specific social effect.

In this chapter, we will look closely at code switching in the Mexican American community. We will consider the various forms of code switching in Mexican American speech in order to shed light on the unique bilingual skill that is required to carry it out effectively. We will also consider the functions of code switching and show how the alternate use of English and Spanish reflects the basic tension between language pride and language panic in the Mexican American **language experience.**

■ The Forms of Code Switching

Linguists have consistently demonstrated that code switching is not simply an erratic mixing of two languages within one discourse. On the contrary, they have shown that speakers tend to be very aware of where, how, and why they code switch. When bilingual speakers code switch, they have a variety of options. A speaker may decide to include a single Spanish word (with Spanish pronunciation) within a stretch of English discourse. A speaker may instead decide to include an entire Spanish phrase within an English sentence or to produce one sentence in Spanish and the other in English. **Intersentential code switching** occurs when the language switch happens at a sentence boundary, as in the following example:

> Anyway, I was in and he was, you know, the one that would let you out.
> And he was laughing cause he saw me coming in. *Se estaba riendo de mí.*
> (He was laughing at me.)

Intrasentential code switching occurs when the speaker switches languages within the boundaries of a single sentence, as in the following example:

> Sí, y luego es una *trampoline* así; pero aquí vienen los ropes así. Y nomás de
> ese tamaño. Esa era para brincar. No era to . . . *it wasn't a big trampoline.*
> (Yes, and there was a trampoline like this, and the ropes were like this. No
> more than this size. That was for jumping. It wasn't a big trampoline.)

Code switching discourse often consists of a **matrix language** and an **embedded language** (Myers-Scotton 1995). The matrix language is the predominant language within a conversation and the embedded language is the intruding language. Pieter Muysken (1995, 180) calls this type of code switching **insertion.** Insertion occurs when a bilingual speaker for any given reason inserts a word, phrase, or sentence from language A in the course of a discourse that is predominantly in language B. One way we can tell that a bilingual is inserting language A material into a language B discourse is the preponderance of language B *system words,* that is, prepositions, inflectional affixes, and so on. Look at the following example of code switched discourse:

> ✳ The mailman delivered the letter to the *viejito* (old man) who sits on the *terraza* (porch).

In this sentence, the predominant language is obviously English and the Spanish words *viejito* and *terraza* are inserted within the English sentence. One reason we can say that the sentence is predominantly English is that the majority of words in the sentence are in English. Another reason to say that it is predominantly English is that the structure of the sentence, that is, the subject, the verb, the prepositions, and so on, create an English grammatical frame.

Consider the following example:

> The mailman, the one who plays *dominó con mi abuelo Agustín en la cantina de la esquina*, delivered the letter to the *viejito* sitting on the *terraza de la casa de mi tía Conce*. (The mailman, the one who plays dominoes with my grandpa at the corner bar, delivered the letter to the old man sitting on the porch of my Aunt Conce's house.)

In this sentence, I count fourteen English words and twenty Spanish words; however, the predominant language still appears to be English. We might at first think this is so because the sentence starts in English. But look at the following sentence:

> *El viejito* sitting on the *terraza de la casa de mi tía Conce* received a letter from the mailman. (The old man sitting on the porch at my Aunt Conce's house received a letter from the mailman.)

What is the predominant language of this sentence? Even though it starts in Spanish, this still appears to be basically an English sentence. Notice that in both cases, the impression we have of English as the predominant language rests primarily on the fact that the grammatical frame of the sentence is in English, even though the sentence may start in Spanish and may contain more Spanish words than English words. The grammatical frame of the sentence is determined by the elements that are more prominent in the hierarchical structure of the sentence. For example, when we have a prepositional phrase like *to the store* the word *to* is more prominent than the phrase *the store*. In fact, the phrase *the store* modifies the preposition *to*. The same can be said of a phrase like *the tall man*. Here *man* is the more prominent word and *the* and *tall* both modify *man*. Insertion, then, occurs when one language tends to occupy the more prominent grammatical positions within the sentence and therefore creates a grammatical frame that is consistent with that language.

It is not always possible to determine a matrix language and an embedded language in code switching, however. Sometimes code switching can appear to be a constant back and forth between two languages, making it difficult to determine a matrix language and an embedded language:

> My sister went to the mall. *Se compró un vestido.* It didn't fit. *Así que la devolvió.* (My sister went to the mall. She bought a dress. It didn't fit. So she returned it.)

Muysken refers to this type of code switching as **alternation** (Muysken 1995, 180). While alternation is most often found in intersentential code switching, it can also occur in intrasentential code switching. Consider the following example:

> My sister *fue al* mall *y se compró un vestido muy* pretty, but it didn't fit *así que* she returned it *al* store *donde la compró.* (My sister went to the mall and bought a dress [that was] very pretty, but it didn't fit so she returned it to the store where she bought it.)

In this sentence, the prominent grammatical positions within the sentence are mixed so that the noun *mall* is dependent on the preposition *al* and the adjective *pretty* is dependent on the noun *vestido*.

Whether they are code switching using an insertion model or an alternation model, bilingual speakers appear to have a tacit knowledge about the kinds of code switching that can exist. If you are bilingual, you may have readily accepted all of the previous examples as easily interpretable. Consider this example, however:

> My sister *fue al* mall *y se* bought *un vestido muy* pretty, but it didn't *quedó así que* she *la* returned *al* store *donde compró* it. (My sister went to the mall and for herself bought a dress very pretty, but it didn't fit, so she it returned to the store where she bought it.)

This sentence is very difficult to understand because it violates some of the unconscious rules that speakers use when they code switch. Shana Poplack explains that "rather than arising from insufficient control of L2 [the speaker's non-dominant language], code switching can be a highly developed skill requiring competence in two languages" (Poplack 1981, 185). Poplack argues that in the same way that monolingual speakers have certain intuitions about their language that allow them to produce an infinite number of well-formed sentences, bilingual speakers also have intuitions about both languages together that allow them to know which parts of a given sentence can be switched and which parts cannot. Poplack proposes two rules that guide bilingual code switching. The first is what she calls "the free morpheme constraint." This rule says that code switching can occur only between words and not within words. It is impossible to switch from one language to another in the middle of a word. The second rule is what she calls "the equivalence constraint." Poplack says that "codes will tend to be switched at points where the juxtaposition of English and Spanish elements does not violate syntactic rules of either language, i.e., at points where the surface structures of the languages map onto each other" (Poplack 1981, 175). This means that switching is impossible at points where the Spanish word order differs from English word order. Consider the following examples:

Ella	le compró		una	nueva	camisa.
She	bought him	a		new	shirt.
A	B		C	D	E

In these sentences, there is equivalence at the points marked with A, B, and C. Within B, however, there is nonequivalence. This nonequivalence results in the impossibility of a switch like "le bought" or "compró him." These two rules show that code switching is, in some sense, highly predictable.

Jacqueline Toribio carried out a study among bilingual speakers from East Los Angeles in which she demonstrated that these rules are strongly adhered to in the Mexican American community. She presented speakers with two stories; the first story, *Snow White and the Seven Dwarfs,* contained code switches that violated Poplack's rules, and the second story, *The Beggar Prince,* contained code switches that did not violate the rules.

Snow White and the Seven Dwarfs

Erase una vez una linda princesita blanca como la nieve. Su madrastra, la reina, tenía un mágico mirror on the wall. The queen often asked, "Who is the más hermosa del valle?" Y un día the mirror answered, "Snow White is the fairest one of all!" Very envious and evil, the reina mandó a un criado que matara a la princesa. El criado la llevó al bosque y out of compassion abandoned la en el bosque. A squirrel took pity on the princess and led her to a pequeña cabina en el monte. En la cabina, vivían siete enanitos que returned to find Snow White asleep in their beds. . . . (Toribio 1999, 121) [Once upon a time there was a beautiful princess as white as snow. Her stepmother, the queen, had a magic mirror on the wall. The queen often asked, "Who is the most beautiful [woman] in the valley?" And one day the mirror answered, "Snow White is the fairest one of all!" Very envious and evil, the queen ordered a servant to kill the princess. The servant took her to the forest and out of compassion abandoned her in the forest. A squirrel took pity on the princess and led her to a small hut in the wilderness. In the hut lived seven dwarves, who returned to find Snow White asleep in their beds.]

The Beggar Prince

El rey Arnulfo tenía una hija muy hermosa que se llamaba Graciela. Al cumplir ella los veinte años, el rey invitó many neighboring princes to a party. Since she was unmarried, he wanted her to choose un esposo. Princess Grace was sweet y cariñosa con todos. Tenía solamente un defecto: she was indecisive. Surrounded by twelve suitors, she could not decide and the king se enojó. Gritó, "¡Juro por Dios que te casaré con el primer hombre that enters this room!" At that exact moment, a beggar, who had evaded a los porteros, entró en la sala. Exclamó, "¡Acabo de oír lo que dijo usted! ¡Juró por Dios! The princess is mine! . . ." (p. 121) [King Arnold had a very beautiful daughter named Grace. When she reached twenty years of age, the king invited many neighboring princes to a party. Since she was unmarried, he wanted her to choose a husband. Princess Grace was sweet and caring with everyone. She had only one fault: she was indecisive. Surrounded by twelve suitors, she could not decide and the king became angry. He shouted, "I swear before God that I will marry you to the first man that enters this room!" At that exact moment, a beggar, who had evaded doormen, entered the room. He exclaimed, "I just heard what you said, Sir! You swore before God! The princess is mine!"]

After they read the stories out loud, she asked her respondents the following questions:

- Was the segment of the fairy tale easy to read? Was it easily understood? Did you enjoy the segment of the fairy tale?

- In comparing the two texts, which one was more easily read? Understood?

- In comparing the two texts, which one did you enjoy best? Why?

- Is there a difference in the type of mixing in each text? (Toribio 1999, 121)

Toribio's respondents clearly noticed the differences between the two texts. One respondent, Yanira, noted that in *Snow White* "too much switching made it confusing. I enjoyed it but was too busy figuring out which language would come next" (Toribio 1999, 121). On the last question, she responded, "There is mixing in *The Beggar Prince*, but it makes sense. *Snow White* changes without a pattern" (Toribio 1999, 121). Another respondent, Guadalupe, said "I liked *The Beggar Prince*. It read more smoothly, I think" (Toribio 1999, 140). Toribio's study clearly shows that bilingual speakers have intuitive knowledge about the formal patterns of code switching.

■ The Functions of Code Switching

Jan-Petter Blom and John Gumperz (1986) carried out a sociolinguistic study of code switching in the small town of Hemnesberget, Norway. In their study, they identified two different functional types of code switching: **situational code switching** and **metaphorical code switching.** Situational code switching refers to a language switch that is motivated by the participant, the topic, or the setting of a conversation. For example, if I am speaking with a bilingual friend and a monolingual friend suddenly joins the conversation, it is quite likely that I may switch languages in order to accommodate the monolingual. If I am having a telephone conversation with someone in my car and arrive at my destination, I may switch languages because I don't feel it is appropriate to use that language in a given place. Both of these examples involve language switches that accompany changes in the conversational setting. However, it is also possible to switch within the same conversational setting. For example, I may be having a conversation in one language and want to refer to something that I normally associate with another language. Consider the following example from Guadalupe Valdés' study:

Pues, sí, mira, cada vez que iba, bueno, la consulta era *eight dollars*. Pero cada vez que iba tenía que comprar las píldoras. Y luego compraba esa cosa que me unto . . . y me salía cada vez que iba como *fifteen* o *twenty dollars*. [Well, yeah, look, every time I went, well, the visit was eight dollars. But every time I had to buy the pills. And then I'd buy the ointment . . . and every time I'd wind up paying like fifteen or twenty dollars.] (Valdés 1976, 66)

This is metaphorical code switching because even though the conversational setting itself does not change, the choice of language reflects, or metaphorically points to, another setting.

Metaphorical code switching adds new **semantic** dimensions to discourse. Rosaura Sánchez argues that "although code switching necessarily implies the use of two codes within the same discourse, this phenomenon must be analyzed as part of the total social, cultural, and linguistic systems of Chicanos" (Sánchez 1994, 139). In making this argument, Sánchez contends that code switching is a discursive resource that "communicates levels of meaning outside the purview of monolingual discourse" (p. 161). Sánchez presents two examples to demonstrate how code switching offers new ways of making meaning for Mexican American speakers:

Mi papá es un *bartender*.
Mi papá es un cantinero. [My father is a bartender.] (Sánchez 1994, 163)

Although the English word *bartender* is semantically equivalent to the Spanish word *cantinero,* the two sentences convey entirely different meanings. Sánchez explains that the word *bartender* is associated with upper strata in the social hierarchy and thus conveys upward social mobility and a high social standing in the community. The word *cantinero,* on the other hand, is associated with the lower strata restricted to the barrio. The first sentence, therefore, differs radically from the second in the connotative meaning it expresses: "My father has a well-paying and well-respected job" as opposed to "my father has a job in the local bar."

Guadalupe Valdés presents a useful typology of code switching that differentiates code switches in terms of the different linguistic motivations that may account for their appearance (Valdés 1976). Her list of motivations includes many factors, such as **lexical gaps, triggering,** and **preformulations.** Valdés proposes that bilingual speakers sometimes code switch because they lack an equivalent word in the language that they are speaking. In other words, they code switch in order to fill a lexical gap. For example, she suggests that the following switches to *trampoline* and *acrobat* both arise from lexical need:

> No, porque, mira, te subes en el *trampoline* y brincas en el aire. Y como brincas bien alto, haces tú la maroma. Como en los *acrobats*. [No, because, look, you get on the trampoline and jump in the air. And since you're jumping so high, you do the somersault like the acrobats.] (Valdés 1976, 59)

When a speaker switches from one language to another to fill a lexical gap, it is possible that the switch may trigger an entire discursive stretch in the second language. Consider the following example:

> No yo sí brincaba en el *trampoline when I was a senior.* Hasta por cierto hasta tenían una de esas chiquitas así. [No I did jump on the trampoline when I was a senior. I even got one of those little ones there.] (Valdés 1976, 58.)

In this example, the speaker switches to *trampoline* in order to fill a lexical gap, then goes on to finish the sentence in English.

Valdés also notes that some code switches occur because they are **fossilized** as linguistic routines, or preformulations. Certain words or phrases tend to carry a special meaning in one language that cannot easily be conveyed in another language. For example, a phrase like *peace and quiet* has a special meaning that differs significantly from *paz y tranquilidad.* Fossilized phrases like this one tend to become linguistic routines, or preformulations, and bilingual speakers may code switch when enacting these routines in order to preserve the intended meaning. The following example shows the speaker switching to the English phrase "not exactly" in order to enact a linguistic routine that, if expressed in Spanish, would perhaps convey a more serious tone that is not consistent with her intended meaning.

> Bueno, *not exactly.* Aquí en *State* dicen que es *co-ed. Not exactly though.* [Well, not exactly. There at State they say it's co-ed. Not exactly though.] (Valdés 1976, 82)

The preceding examples show how bilingual speakers may code switch for linguistic reasons such as the existence of a lexical gap in one language, the triggering effect of lexical insertion, or the semantic charge of linguistic routines. In addition, bilingual speakers often code switch for reasons that arise within the interaction frameworks where speech takes place. Carol Myers-Scotton presents a useful model for analyzing the social motivations for code switching. She contends that code switches are intimately bound up with the **rights and obligations sets** that emerge in linguistic interaction. A rights and obligations set is "an abstract construct, derived from situational factors, standing for the attitudes and expectations of participants towards one another" (Myers-Scotton 1993, 85). The choice of one language or another in discourse, then, serves either to conform to the attitudes and expectations of other speakers involved in the conversation or to change those attitudes and expectations. We will look at each of these possibilities in turn.

Code switching sometimes occurs because there is a shift in the perceived rights and obligations set in the course of a conversation. Myers-Scotton presents an example from Nairobi, where there is extensive code switching between Swahili and Luyia. In her example, a security guard is conversing with a visitor in Swahili. Once the security guard discovers that the visitor comes from his hometown, the conversation switches to Luyia. Myers-Scotton observes that "the content of the factor 'ethnicity' changes from unknown to shared and the . . . rights and obligations set changes from that holding between strangers to that holding between ethnic brethren" (p. 114). These situational code switches are frequent in the Mexican American community and reflect the ways in which bilingual speakers enact linguistic dexterity in order to conform to the social expectations inherent in a speech event. Such social expectations may include the presence of a different interlocutor or of new information about the same interlocutor. Social expectations may also include changes in topic. For example, the following interaction between a Puerto Rican executive and his secretary shows how Spanish is associated with the Puerto Rican parade:

Executive: Sincerely, Luis González.
Secretary: Do you have the enclosures for the letter, Mr. González?
Executive: Oh yes, here they are.
Secretary: OK.
Executive: Ah, this man William Bolger got his organization to contribute a lot of money to the Puerto Rican parade. He's very much for it. *¿Tú fuiste a la parada?* [Did you go to the parade?]
Secretary: *Sí, yo fui.* [Yes, I went.]

Executive:	¿Sí? [Yes?]
Secretary:	Uh huh.
Executive:	Y ¿cómo te estuvo? [And how did you like it?] (Auer 1995, 117–18)

When the executive brings up the subject of the Puerto Rican parade, the conversation suddenly switches completely to Spanish.

Speakers may also use code switching in order to change the rights and obligations set within a conversation. Peter Auer introduces the concept of **language negotiation,** which often occurs in situations of **dynamic bilingualism.** He argues that "language choice often ties up with individual histories of interaction in which patterns of language choice may have developed, or is simply a matter of individual preferences, which are, in turn, related to linguistic competencies and personal linguistic biographies, as well as to complex matters of bi-cultural identity" (Auer 1995, 127). In these cases, speakers use code switching to change the rights and obligations set of a conversation from what it presently is to what they expect it to be.

Sánchez offers a compelling example of this type of language negotiation. "In the presence of speakers of 'standard' varieties of Spanish, some Chicanos will shift immediately to English lest they be criticized for particular conjugations or word choices. This type of code-shifting reflects the social standing of the Spanish varieties spoken in the Southwest and the disdain with which these are viewed by educated Mexicans, Latin Americans, and other Hispanics" (Sánchez 1994, 150–51). Mexican American speakers, then, use code switching in order to change the rights and obligations sets that emerge in particular conversational exchanges. The agential role of speakers in code switching discourse does not always take place in the context of insider-outsider encounters, however. Bilingual speakers may also change rights and obligations sets in conversations with peers and family members. Consider the following exchange among the members of a Mexican American family in El Paso, in which one daughter is complaining about her food:

Daughter 1:	Ah, it's hot.
Daughter 2:	Here you are. . . .
Daughter 1:	Does it taste good with butter on top? . . . Doesn't taste like nothing to me!
Mother:	A ver, deja probarlo. [Look, try it.]

Daughter 1:	You know what it tastes like?
Grandma:	Sabe a lo que le pongan arriba. [You know what they put on top.]
Daughter 1:	That, that stuff my mom makes. What's it called?
Daughter 2:	No, no he comido. [No. I haven't eaten it.]
Daughter 1:	It's soft like this, like. . . .
Grandma:	Pos, si le pones sal arriba, sabe a esa sal arriba, si le pones crema, pos a crema. [Look, if you put salt on it, you know, it tastes like salt; if you put sour cream on it, it tastes like sour cream.]
Daughter 2:	Tú nomás frijoles y carne. Ni ensalada te apuesto que te has servido. [All you ever eat is beans and meat. I'll bet you don't even eat salad.]
Mother:	No, nada. [No, nothing.] (Sánchez 1994, 147–48)

Notice in this exchange that Daughter 1 continually speaks in English even when being addressed in Spanish by her mother and grandma. The exchanges between Daughter 1 and Daughter 2 begin in English. However, as the conversation unfolds, Daughter 2 begins to address Daughter 1 in Spanish. The shift from English to Spanish serves to indicate a change in the rights and obligations set obtained in the conversational exchange. While at the beginning of the conversation, Daughter 2 responded in English to Daughter 1 as a sign of solidarity, the ensuing switch to Spanish enacts a break in that solidarity. Sánchez explains this episode stating that "an English intervention would sound like support for [Daughter 1's] carrying-on, as it would place her at a peer level. Her negative reply in Spanish is meant to put a stop to her sister's insistence" (Sánchez 1994, 149–50). Thus, the use of code switching reflects a change from a rights and obligations set where sibling solidarity is present to a rights and obligations set where one daughter "assumes the role of a 'wiser' sister and is reinforced by her mother who agrees with her appraisal" (Sánchez 1994, 150).

Code switching can thus serve to change or to conform to the specific rights and obligations sets that emerge in conversational settings. In bilingual communities, however, code switching is often itself part of the rights and obligations set in a given conversational event. For example, in her study of code switching among women in Córdova, New Mexico, María Dolores Gonzales suggests that "when the borders of certain speech communities become blurred, the blending of Spanish and English follows. A third code—a hybrid or by-product of Spanish and English—is created and becomes integrated as a viable and socially accepted language code among its speakers and hearers. I refer to this process as language hybridity" (Gonzales 1999, 26). In an example taken from a bridal shower in Córdova, she shows how code switching itself becomes an integral part of the rights and obligations set that is encountered in the conversational exchange.

Woman 1: Always be ready to go with him.
Woman 2: Hazle frijoles todos los días, que es la mejor comida. [Make him beans every day, because that is the best food.]
Mother: Hazle frijoles todos los días. [Make him beans every day.]
Bride: He likes frijoles. Le gustan los frijoles y las tortillas. [He likes beans and tortillas.] We're on our way.
Woman 4: Give him three hugs and three kisses a day.
Bride: That's a good one. I like that one.
Woman 5: Que no deje su marido ir solo para dondequiera: que se esté junto de ella. [Don't let your husband go anywhere alone. Make sure he's with you.]
Bride: I already. . . . Ese sí me acuerdo. [Yes, I agree with that.]
Mother: Ese sí te gustó. [You like that.]
Bride: Ese me gustó mucho. [I like that a lot.]
Woman 5: You better believe it. (Gonzales 1999, 34)

In this example, the rights and obligations set that obtains would appear to admit both languages. The task of giving advice is carried out in both languages. Notice that the advice to keep a close eye on her husband is expressed in Spanish initially ("Que no deje su marido ir solo para dondequiera: que se esté junto de ella"), but the rejoinder—"You better believe it"—is expressed in English. Not only is code switching accepted in this context, it is also expected. Gonzales explains, "I attribute this innovative behavior to the strong sense of in-group cohesiveness and security that permits the respondents to cross social, cultural, and linguistic borders . . . in the process they alter their communal language behavior without feeling a threat to their sense of identity" (Gonzales 1999, 35). This sense of cohesiveness extends well beyond the conversational setting. The billboard in figure 8, for example, makes use of code switching to signal in-group cohesiveness with the target market of Mexican Americans.

■ 8. A billboard uses code switching as a symbol of in-group cohesiveness. (Photograph by Glenn Martínez)

Concluding Thoughts

In this chapter we have considered the language practices of code switching in the Mexican American community. We have seen that despite the disparaging attitudes toward code switching among monolingual English speakers, this practice is a viable and vital part of Mexican American communication that reflects a very keen command of both languages. We looked first at the form of code switching, giving an idea of the very complex nature of the practice. Speakers display their linguistic dexterity in managing this complexity. They also hold precise intuitive knowledge about the patterns of code switching. We then looked at the various functions of code switching in Mexican American speech. First, Mexican American speakers use code switching in order to fulfill certain linguistic functions that are part and parcel of the reality of being bilingual. Code switching is used to fill lexical gaps, to preserve the force of linguistic routines, and in triggered response to other code switches. In addition, however, code switching is used to fulfill social functions. In particular, it is reflective of the rights and obligations sets that obtain in distinct conversational settings. Bilingual speakers can use code switching either to conform to a certain rights and obligations set or to challenge and resist it. Finally, within bilingual communities it is also common that code switching itself is indexed with a conventionalized rights and obligations set. In other words, code switching can in and of itself become the expected norm in conversational settings among Mexican American bilinguals.

■ Discussion Exercises

1. Explain the difference between insertion and alternation.

2. How does a situational code switch differ from a metaphorical code switch?

3. Think of a linguistic routine that you often use in English. What is its equivalent in Spanish? Would you use this equivalent in a casual conversation? Why or why not?

4. How do bilinguals use code switching in order to accommodate a rights and obligations set already in place in a conversation?

5. How do bilinguals use code switching to change a rights and obligations set already in place in a conversation?

6. Make a list of five sentences with intrasentential code switches. Try to determine what linguistic motivations account for the code switches.

7. Identify three conversational settings in which the rights and obligations set that obtains calls for code switching as the normal medium of conversational exchange. Who are the participants? Where do these conversations take place? What kinds of topics come up in the conversation?

■ Suggested Readings

Auer, J. C. P. *Bilingual Conversation*. Philadelphia: John Benjamins, 1984.

Galindo, D. Leticia, and María Dolores Gonzales. *Speaking Chicana: Voice, Power, and Identity*. Tucson: University of Arizona Press, 1999.

Myers-Scotton, Carol. *Social Motivations for Code Switching: Evidence from Africa*. Oxford: Oxford University Press, 1993.

Sánchez, Rosaura. *Chicano Discourse*. Houston: Arte Público Press, 1994.

7

Conclusion

I n this book, we have examined the Mexican American language experience from multiple perspectives. This multidimensional approach reflects the complexity of language in the Mexican American community. We began our analysis of the Mexican American language experience by focusing on the ideas and ideologies surrounding language both inside and outside of the Mexican American community. In this discussion, we identified two opposing ideologies that grate on the tongues of Mexican Americans throughout the United States. On the one hand, we looked at the ideology of language panic, in which the language of Mexican Americans is looked down upon as some sort of degenerate variety and as inferior to the dominant language. Its opposite is the ideology of language pride, in which Mexican Americans view their language as a viable and valuable means of expressing their interests, feelings, beliefs, and identities. The tension between these conflicting ideologies is fundamental to the Mexican American language experience.

We then looked at language attitudes and at language shift in the Mexican American community, and once again saw how the tension between language panic and language pride shapes the way speakers think about the language and their ultimate decision to change language behaviors. In the ensuing chapters, we saw how the fundamental tension between language panic and language pride can also have repercussions on the multiple ways that speakers use their language. We considered sociolinguistic discontinuities in Mexican American Spanish that become manifest in areas such as linguistic proficiency, linguistic style, and linguistic identity. At the same time, we considered the growing vitality of English in Mexican American verbal behavior. Many sources converge on Mexican American English, reflecting the complex status of the community as an ethnic and linguistic minority. Finally, we examined Mexican American code switching, a verbal practice that may offer Mexican American speakers a performative means of attenuating conflictive language ideologies.

As we have seen throughout this survey, the inherent complexity of the

Mexican American language experience resists simplification. This may be one of the reasons why language issues continue to stir up controversy in practically every facet of Mexican American social life. The purpose of this book is to underscore this complexity and to invite you to continue to explore how this complexity can be channeled to find more appropriate solutions to the many social problems that continue to plague the Mexican American community because of its ethnic and linguistic minority status in the United States. Educational issues such as the methods of bilingual education at the elementary and secondary levels and the teaching of Spanish as a heritage language at the high school and college levels are in desperate need of new perspectives that can offer fresh solutions capable of simultaneously achieving the desired educational outcomes and the moral demands of social justice. Health-care issues such as the lack of access to quality health care because of language barriers are also in need of new solutions that are capable of communicating essential information on disease awareness and prevention within the context of a complex language experience. Legal issues such as the use of linguistic profiling in order to deny equal access to affordable housing or well-paying jobs must also be addressed in ways that are sensitive to the complexity of the Mexican American language experience.

I hope that after reading this book you will become more aware of the central role of language in Mexican American life and that you will want to continue studying this vital aspect of Mexican American studies. At the same time, I hope that in doing so you can use and apply that knowledge in ways that will benefit and ultimately transform our community.

◼ GLOSSARY

alternation: A type of code switching in which both languages share equal grammatical prominence.

archaism: A word, phrase, or sound that was once widely used in many varieties of a language but has subsequently become restricted to a limited number of more or less isolated varieties.

bilingual continuum: A gradient concept of bilingualism where each language is seen as more or less dominant over the other. Speakers may move back and forth along the bilingual continuum throughout the course of their lives.

borrowing: A word that is taken from language B and phonetically adapted to the sound system of language A. For example, the word *troca* is a borrowed term derived from *truck* and the word *jaina* is a borrowed term derived from *honey.*

calque: The assigning of a new meaning to a word in language A that is phonetically similar to a word in language B. For example, the Spanish word *carpeta* had an original meaning of 'notebook'. In contact with English, however, the word *carpeta* has been assigned the new meaning 'rug' based on the phonetic similarity with the English word *carpet.*

code switching: The alternate use of two languages, normally in one sentence, but it can also be used to describe two languages being used in one unit of discourse.

covert prestige: Positive attitudes toward generally stigmatized linguistic features or behaviors that are normally expressed implicitly through use rather than explicitly through direct expressions of support.

dialogism: Discourse that is shaped by the ongoing interaction of the participants.

diglossia: Socially or institutionally sanctioned patterns of language choice that dictate the functional domains in which each language is used.

dynamic bilingualism: A situation in which a large proportion of the members of a speech community are bilingual and where the social norms that govern the use of one language or the other are not fixed. Instead, speakers choose to use one language or the other on the basis of individual preferences and communicative demands.

embedded language: In code switching, the embedded language is the language of the material that is introduced into the discourse of the predominant (or matrix) language.

ethnolinguistic vitality: A theory that seeks to explain the survival or demise of languages in competition on the basis of the economic, demographic, and sociohistoric variables that make a group likely to behave as a distinctive and active collective entity in intergroup relations.

fossilization: The blurring of meaningful grammatical morphemes within a frequently occurring word form. For example, the independent meaning of the imperfect ending in—*ía* is often fossilized in frequently occurring words such as *había*. That is, the verb *haber* is typically used with the *-ía* inflection, so speakers tend to use *había* even when another form of the verb would be grammatically more appropriate.

functional domain: A discursive site—which may include a topic, a person, or a place—in which a language is used to accomplish a communicative function. For example, school is a functional domain which many Mexican Americans reserve for English, so talking about math or physics in Spanish becomes rather difficult. Similarly, making tamales is a functional domain which many Mexican Americans reserve for Spanish, so talking about making them in English is somewhat difficult.

genre: A particular configuration of discourse features that correlates with the enactment of a specific social action.

insertion: A type of code switching in which one language has greater grammatical prominence than the other.

intersentential code switching: Code switching that occurs between sentence boundaries.

intrasentential code switching: Code switching that occurs within the boundaries of a sentence.

language attrition: The gradual loss of linguistic proficiency by an individual due to restricted use of one language in favor of another language.

language experience: The composite of a group's experience with, in, and through language.

language ideology: A set of beliefs about language articulated by users as a rationalization or justification of perceived language structure and use.

language maintenance: The successful transmission of a language across generations.

language negotiation: The use of code switching in order to force an interlocutor into choosing one language over another.

language shift: The declining use of one language in favor of another over a period of generations. An example would be a family where the grandparents speak only Spanish, the parents are bilingual in English and Spanish, and the children speak only English.

lexical gap: A linguistic motivation for code switching in which the lack of a particular word in one language induces the expression of the word in another language.

lexicon: The set of words that are said to belong to a language, the vocabulary of a language.

linguistic capital: The idea that language use has an inherent value. Linguistic capital is a cornerstone of the marketing of English self-teaching programs in the United States.

matched-guise test: A language attitude elicitation technique in which respondents are confronted with concrete linguistic evidence—such as a tape recording—and asked to provide subjective evaluations of those facts.

matrix language: In code switching, the matrix language is the language that is grammatically prominent.

metaphorical code switching: Code switching that indirectly or metaphorically points to a change in situation.

morphology: The study of the structure of words in a language. Morphologists study how suffixes and roots combine to make words and how words can be put together to make new words.

over-coding: A linguistic process in which a word is assigned a different meaning based on its syntactic (grammatical) position and its phonetic similarity with another word. For example, Chicano caló speakers can respond in the affirmative by saying *simon* instead of *sí*.

overt prestige: Positive attitudes toward linguistic features or behaviors that are normally expressed explicitly even if they are not adhered to in use.

phonology: The study of the sound system of a language. Phonologists study how and why pronunciations of words differ within languages and from one language variety to another.

preformulations: Linguistic routines in which the collocation of the words carries a unique meaning distinct from the words separately. Examples are the English phrase *peace and quiet* or the Spanish phrase *con el favor de Dios*. These phrases lose much of their semantic force when translated.

recontact: A situation of sustained interaction between speakers who are at different points in the process of language shift; recontact can result in a reversal and a rethreading of the language shift process itself.

rights and obligations set: A concept encompassing the attitudes and expectations of participants in a conversation toward one another in a particular situation.

semantics: The study of systems of meaning in a language. Semanticists study the componential structure of word meaning and the ways that word meanings interrelate in natural languages.

situational code switching: Code switching that occurs in response to a change in the conversational setting; that is, location, participants, or topic.

social network: The sum of interpersonal ties among individuals in a social arena.

sociolinguistic discontinuities: Linguistic differences between members of a speech community that reflect dynamic categories such as the speaker's network of social relations or desire to belong to a particular group or "community of practice."

sociolinguistic interview: An instrument for eliciting linguistic data in which an interviewer engages an interviewee in casual conversation over a sustained period of time.

sociolinguistic questionnaire: A list of closed-ended questions normally measured on a graded scale. This instrument is often used to elicit language attitudes.

stable bilingualism: A situation where all members of a speech community are bilingual. These members are also aware of the different appropriate functions of each language, so they would never use language A in domain B or language B in domain A.

syntax: The study of the sentence structure of a language. Syntacticians study how different words are used to create particular constructions, such as questions, in a language.

transitional bilingualism: A situation in which one language systematically loses its domains of use over the course of several generations.

triggering: In code switching, when the presence of one word or phrase in a particular language leads to the switching of other words and phrases into that language.

vernacularization: The process by which a community of second-language learners nativize certain features of that language. Indian English, for example, is often considered a vernacularized variety of English.

vestigial bilingualism: A situation where fragments of one language persist with no real communicative value. All communication is achieved in the second language.

■ BIBLIOGRAPHY

Aparicio, Frances. 2000. "Of Spanish Dispossessed." In *Language Ideologies: Critical Perspectives on the Official English Movement.* Vol. 1, eds. Roseann Dueñas González and Ildikó Melis, 248–75. Mahwah, NJ: Lawrence Erlbaum Associates.

Attinasi, John. 1985. "Hispanic Attitudes in Northwest Indiana and New York." In *Spanish Language Use and Public Life in the United States,* eds. Lucía Elías-Olivares, Elizabeth A. Leone, Rene Cisneros, and John R. Gutiérrez, 27–58. Berlin: Mouton.

Auer, J. C. P. 1984. *Bilingual Conversation.* Philadelphia: John Benjamins.

———. 1995. "The Pragmatics of Code-Switching: A Sequential Approach." In *One Speaker, Two Languages: Cross-disciplinary Perspectives on Code Switching,* eds. Leslie Milroy and Pieter Muysken, 115–35. Cambridge: Cambridge University Press.

Baker, Colin. 1992. *Attitudes and Language.* Clevedon, U.K.: Multilingual Matters.

Bergen, John J., ed. 1990. *Spanish in the United States: Sociolinguistic Issues.* Washington, DC: Georgetown University Press.

Bergen, John J., and Erlinda Gonzales-Berry. 1989. "Attitudes, Proficiency, and Perceived Discrimination among New Mexico Spanish Speakers." In *Mexican American Spanish in Its Societal and Cultural Contexts,* eds. Dennis J. Bixler-Márquez, Jacob L. Ornstein-Galicia, and George K. Green, 171–88. Brownsville: University of Texas at Brownsville.

Bernal-Enríquez, Ysaura. 2000. "Factores socio-históricos en la pérdida del español del suroeste en los Estados Unidos y sus implicaciones para la revitalización." In *Research on Spanish in the United States: Linguistic Issues and Challenges,* ed. Ana Roca, 121–36. Somerville, MA: Cascadilla Press.

Bills, Garland, Alan Hudson, and Eduardo Hernández-Chávez. 2000. "Spanish Home Language Use and English Proficiency as Differential Measures of Language Maintenance and Shift." *Southwest Journal of Linguistics* 19: 11–28.

Binder, Norman. 1989. "Attitudes towards Language Use: A Multi-Group Analysis." In *Mexican American Spanish in Its Societal and Cultural Contexts,* eds. Dennis J. Bixler-Márquez, Jacob L. Ornstein-Galicia, and George K. Green, 165–70. Brownsville: University of Texas at Brownsville.

Bixler-Márquez, Dennis J., Jacob L. Ornstein-Galicia, and George K. Green. 1989. *Mexican American Spanish in Its Societal and Cultural Contexts.* Brownsville: University of Texas at Brownsville.

Blom, Jan-Petter, and John Gumperz. 1986. "Social Meaning in Linguistic Structures: Code-Switching in Norway." In *Directions in Sociolinguistics,* eds. John Gumperz and Dell Hymes, 407–734. Cambridge, MA: Blackwell.

Bloomfield, Leonard. 1933. *Language.* Chicago: University of Chicago Press.

Bowen, J. Donald, and Jacob L. Ornstein, eds. 1976. *Studies in Southwest Spanish.* Rowley, MA: Newbury House.

Braybrooke, David. 1967. "Ideology." In *The Encyclopedia of Philosophy.* Vol. 3, ed. Paul Edwards, 124–27. New York: Macmillan.

Briggs, Charles L. 1988. *Competence in Performance: The Creativity of Tradition in Mexicano Verbal Art.* Philadelphia: University of Pennsylvania Press.

Brutt-Griffler, Janina. 2002. *World English: A Study of Its Development.* Clevedon, U.K.: Multilingual Matters.

Burciaga, José Antonio. 1988. *Weedee Peepo.* Edinburg: University of Texas–Pan American Press.

Calvet, Louis-Jean. 1998. *Language Wars and Linguistic Politics,* trans. Michel Petheram. Oxford: Oxford University Press.

Cashman, Holly. 2001. "Doing Being Bilingual: Language Maintenance, Language Shift, and Conversational Code-Switching in Southwest Detroit." Ph.D. dissertation, University of Michigan, Ann Arbor.

Cisneros, Rene, and Elizabeth Leone. 1983. "Mexican American Language Communities in the Twin Cities: An Example of Contact and Recontact." In *Spanish in the U.S. Setting: Beyond the Southwest,* ed. Lucía Elías-Olivares, 181–210. Rosslyn, VA: National Clearinghouse for Bilingual Education.

de la Torre, Adela, and Antonio Estrada. 2001. *Mexican Americans and Health: ¡Sana! ¡Sana!* Tucson: University of Arizona Press.

Doran, Amanda. 2001. "Language Use and Identity in a Bilingual Community: Re-Examining the English of Mexican Americans." Ph.D. dissertation, University of Texas at Austin.

Eagleton, Terry. 1991. *Ideology: An Introduction.* London: Verso.

Edwards, John. 1994. *Multilingualism.* New York: Penguin.

Elías-Olivares, Lucía, Elizabeth A. Leone, Rene Cisneros, and John R. Gutiérrez. 1985. *Spanish Language Use and Public Life in the United States.* Berlin: Mouton.

Fasold, Ralph W. 1987. *The Sociolinguistics of Society.* Cambridge, MA: Blackwell.

Fernández, Rosa. 1988. "Future Directions for Research on Speech Attitudes." In *Research Issues and Problems in United States Spanish,* eds. Jacob L. Ornstein-Galicia, George K. Green, and Dennis J. Bixler-Márquez, 111–24. Brownsville, TX: Pan American University at Brownsville.

———. 1990. "Actitudes hacia los cambios de códigos en Nuevo México: reacciones de un sujeto a ejemplos de su habla." In *Spanish in the United States: Sociolinguistic Issues,* ed. John Bergen, 49–58. Washington, DC: Georgetown University Press.

Flores, Juan, and George Yúdice. 1997. "Living Borders/*Buscando América:* Latino Languages of Self-Formation." In *Latinos and Education,* eds. Antonia Darder, Rodolfo D. Torres, and Henry Gutiérrez, 190–91. New York: Routledge.

Floyd, Mary Beth. 1982. "Spanish Language Maintenance in Colorado." In *Bilingualism and Language Contact,* eds. Florence Barkin, Elizabeth A. Brandt, and Jacob L. Ornstein-Galicia. New York: Teachers College Press.

Fought, Carmen. 2003. *Chicano English in Context.* New York: Palgrave.

Fromkin, Victoria, and Robert Rodman. 1988. *An Introduction to Language*. 4th ed. New York: Holt, Rinehart, and Winston.

Gal, Susan. 1979. *Language Shift: Social Determinants of Linguistic Change in Bilingual Austria*. New York: Academic Press.

Galindo, D. Leticia. 1987. "Linguistic Influence and Variation on the English of Chicano Adolescents in Austin, Texas." Ph.D. dissertation, University of Texas at Austin.

Galindo, D. Leticia, and María Dolores Gonzales, eds. 1999. *Speaking Chicana: Voice, Power, and Identity*. Tucson: University of Arizona Press.

García, Maryellen. 1982. "Syntactic Variation in Verb Phrases of Motion in U.S.–Mexican Spanish." In *Spanish in the United States: Sociolinguistic Aspects*, eds. Jon Amastae and Lucía Elías-Olivares, 82–92. Cambridge: Cambridge University Press.

———. 2003. "Speaking Spanish in Los Angeles and San Antonio: Who, When, Where, Why." *Southwest Journal of Linguistics* 22: 1–22.

García, Ofelia. 1995. "Spanish Language Loss as a Determinant of Income among Latinos in the United States." In *Power and Inequality in Language Education*, ed. James W. Tollefson, 142–60. Cambridge: Cambridge University Press.

Giles, Howard, Richard Y. Bourhis, and Donald M. Taylor. 1977. "Toward a Theory of Language in Ethnic Group Relations." In *Language, Ethnicity, and Intergroup Relations*, ed. Howard Giles. 307–48. New York: Academic Press.

Gonzales, María Dolores. 1999. "Crossing Social and Cultural Borders: The Road to Language Hybridity." In *Speaking Chicana: Voice, Power, and Identity*, eds. D. Leticia Galindo and María Dolores, 13–38. Tucson: University of Arizona Press.

González, Arturo. 2002. *Mexican Americans and the U.S. Economy: Quest for Buenos Días*. Tucson: University of Arizona Press.

González, Norma. 2001. *I Am My Language: Discourses of Women and Children in the Borderlands*. Tucson: University of Arizona Press.

González, Roseann Dueñas, and Ildikó Melis. 2000. *Language Ideologies: Critical Perspectives on the Official English Movement*. Vol. 1. Mahwah, NJ: Lawrence Erlbaum Associates.

———. 2001. *Language Ideologies: Critical Perspectives on the Official English Movement*. Vol. 2. Mahwah, NJ: Lawrence Erlbaum Associates.

Grosjean, François. 1982. *Life with Two Languages: An Introduction to Bilingualism*. Cambridge, MA: Harvard University Press.

Gutiérrez, Manuel. 1996. "Tendencias y alternancias en la expresión de condicionalidad en el español hablado en Houston." *Hispania* 79: 567–77.

Haarmann, Harold. 1986. *Language in Ethnicity: A View of Basic Ecological Relations*. Berlin: Mouton de Gruyter.

Hidalgo, Margarita. 1984. *Language Attitudes and Language Use in Cd. Juárez, Mexico*. El Paso: Center for Inter-American and Border Studies.

———. 1989. "Perceptions of Spanish-English Code-Switching in Juárez, Mexico." In

Mexican American Spanish in Its Societal and Cultural Contexts, eds. Dennis J. Bixler-Márquez, Jacob L. Ornstein-Galicia, and George K. Green, 131–50. Brownsville: University of Texas at Brownsville.

———. 1993. "The Dialectics of Spanish Language Loyalty and Maintenance on the U.S.–Mexico border: A Two-Generation Study." In *Spanish in the United States: Linguistic Contact and Diversity,* eds. Ana Roca and John M. Lipski, 47–74. Berlin: Mouton de Gruyter.

Hill, Jane. 2001. "The Racializing Function of Language Panics." In *Language Ideologies: Critical Perspectives on the Official English Movement.* Vol. 2, eds. Roseann Dueñas González and Ildikó Melis, 245–67, Mahwah, NJ: Lawrence Erlbaum Associates.

Holmes, Janet. 1992. *An Introduction to Sociolinguistics.* London: Longman.

House, Boyce. 1943. *I Give You Texas: 500 Jokes of the Lone Star State.* San Antonio: Naylor Co.

Hudson, Alan, Eduardo Hernández-Chávez, and Garland Bills. 1995. "The Many Faces of Language Maintenance: Spanish Language Claiming in Five Southwestern States." In *Spanish in Four Continents,* ed. Carmen Silva-Corvalán, 165–83. Washington, DC: Georgetown University Press.

Hudson, Richard A. 1980. *Sociolinguistics.* Cambridge: Cambridge University Press.

Hudson-Edwards, Alan, and Garland Bills. 1980. "Intergenerational language Shift in an Albuquerque Barrio." In *Festschrift for Jacob Ornstein: Studies in General Linguistics and Sociolinguistics,* eds. Edward L. Blansitt Jr. and Richard V. Teschner, 139–58. Rowley, MA: Newbury House.

Irvine, Judith T., and Susan Gal. 2000. "Language Ideology and Linguistic Differentiation." In *Regimes of Language: Ideologies, Polities, and Identities,* ed. Paul V. Kroskrity. Santa Fe, NM: School of American Research Press.

Jaramillo, June. 1995. "The Passive Legitimization of Spanish. A Macrosociolinguistic Study of a Quasi-Border: Tucson, Arizona." *International Journal of the Sociology of Language* 114: 67–91.

Jaramillo, June, and Garland Bills. 1982. "The Phoneme /ch/ in the Spanish of Tomé, New Mexico." In *Bilingualism and Language Contact: Spanish, English, and Native American Languages,* eds. Florence Barkin, Elizabeth A. Brandt, and Jacob L. Ornstein-Galicia, 154–65. New York: Teachers College Press.

Kachru, Braj B. 1986. *The Alchemy of English: The Spread, Functions, and Models of Non-native Englishes.* Urbana: University of Illinois Press.

Katz, Linda Fine. 1974. "The Evolution of the Pachuco Language and Culture." Master's Thesis, University of California at Los Angeles.

Kravitz, Merryl. 1989. "Decisions of Correctness in New Mexico Spanish." In *Mexican American Spanish in Its Societal and Cultural Contexts,* eds. Dennis J. Bixler-Márquez, Jacob L. Ornstein-Galicia, and George K. Green, 151–64. Brownsville: University of Texas at Brownsville.

Kroskrity, Paul V., ed. 2000. *Regimes of Language: Ideologies, Polities, and Identities.* Santa Fe, NM: School of American Research Press.

Labov, William. 1972. *Language in the Inner City: Studies in the Black English Vernacular.* Philadelphia: University of Pennsylvania Press.

Landry, Rodrique, and Richard Y. Bourhis. 1997. "Linguistic Landscape and Ethnolinguistic Vitality: An Empirical Study." *Journal of Language and Social Psychology* 16: 23–49.

López Morales, Humberto. 1993. *Sociolingüística.* 2nd ed. Madrid: Gredos.

MacGregor-Mendoza, Patricia. 1998. "Language and the Bilingual Teacher: Use, Attitudes, Roles." *Southwest Journal of Linguistics* 17: 83–100.

McGuire, William J. 1985. "Attitudes and Attitude Change." In *Handbook of Social Psychology.* Vol. 3, eds. Gardner Lindzey and Elliott Aronson, 248. New York: Random House.

Mejías, Hugo, Pamela Anderson-Mejías, and Ralph Carlson. 2003. "Attitude Update: Spanish on the South Texas Border." *Hispania* 86: 138–50.

Mendoza-Denton, Norma. 1999. "Fighting Words: Latina Girls, Gangs, and Language Attitudes." In *Speaking Chicana: Voice, Power, and Identity,* eds. D. Leticia Galindo and María Dolores Gonzales, 39–58. Tucson: University of Arizona Press.

Metcalf, Allan. 1974. "The Study of California Chicano English." *International Journal of the Sociology of Language* 2: 53–58.

Muysken, Pieter. 1995. "Code-Switching and Grammatical Theory." In *One Speaker, Two Languages: Cross-disciplinary Perspectives on Code Switching,* eds. Leslie Milroy and Pieter Muysken, 177–98. Cambridge: Cambridge University Press.

Myers-Scotton, Carol. 1993. *Social Motivations for Code-Switching.* Oxford: Oxford University Press.

———. 1995. "A Lexically Based Model of Code-Switching." In *One Speaker, Two Languages: Cross-disciplinary Perspectives on Code Switching,* eds. Leslie Milroy and Pieter Muysken, 233–66. Cambridge: Cambridge University Press.

Ochoa, Gilda. 2004. *Becoming Neighbors in a Mexican American Community.* Austin: University of Texas Press.

Ornstein-Galicia, Jacob L. 1988. *Form and Function in Chicano English.* Malabar, FL: Robert Krieger Publishing.

Ornstein-Galicia, Jacob, George K. Green, and Dennis J. Bixler-Márquez. 1988. *Research Issues and Problems in United States Spanish.* Brownsville: Pan American University at Brownsville.

Peñalosa, Fernando. 1980. *Chicano Sociolinguistics.* Rowley, MA: Newbury House.

Penfield, Joyce, and Jacob Ornstein-Galicia. 1985. *Chicano English: An Ethnic Contact Dialect.* Amsterdam: John Benjamins.

Phillips, Robert N., Jr. 1975. "Variations in Los Angeles Spanish Phonology." In *El Lenguaje de los Chicanos: Regional and Social Characteristics Used by Mexican Ameri-*

cans, eds. Eduardo Hernández-Chavez, Andrew D. Cohen, and Anthony F. Beltramo, 52–60. Arlington, VA: Center for Applied Linguistics.

Poplack, Shana. 1981. "Syntactic Structure and the Social Function of Code Switching." In *Latino Language and Communicative Behavior,* ed. Richard P. Durán, 169–84. Norwood, NJ: Ablex.

———. 1982. "Sometimes I'll Start in Spanish *y Termino en Español:* Toward a Typology of Code-Switching." In *Spanish in the United States: Sociolinguistic Aspects,* eds. Jon Amastae and Lucía Elías-Olivares, 230–63. Cambridge: Cambridge University Press.

Portes, Alejandro, and Rubén G. Rumbaut. 1996. *Immigrant America: A Portrait.* Berkeley: University of California Press.

Ramírez, Arnulfo. 1992. *El Español de los Estados Unidos: El lenguaje de los hispanos.* Madrid: Editorial Mapfre.

Ramírez, K. 1973. "Lexical Usage and Attitude toward Southwest Spanish in the Ysleta, Texas Area." *Hispania* 56: 308–15.

Rivera-Mills, Susana. 2000. "Intra-ethnic Attitudes among Hispanics in a Northern California Community." In *Research on Spanish in the United States: Linguistic Issues and Challenges,* ed. Ana Roca, 377–89. Somerville, MA: Cascadilla Press.

Roca, Ana. 2000 *Research on Spanish in the United States: Linguistic Issues and Challenges.* Somerville, MA: Cascadilla Press.

Roca, Ana, and John M. Lipski. 1993. *Spanish in the United States: Linguistic Contact and Diversity.* Berlin: Mouton de Gruyter.

Salazar, Rubén. 1995. *Border Correspondent: Selected Writings, 1955–1970,* ed. Mario T. García. Berkeley: University of California Press.

Sánchez, Rosaura. 1994. *Chicano Discourse.* Houston: Arte Público Press.

Santa Ana, Otto. 1991. "Phonetic Simplification Processes in the English of the Barrio: A Cross-generational Sociolinguistic Study of the Chicanos of Los Angeles." Ph.D. dissertation, University of Pennsylvania, Philadelphia.

———. 1993. "Chicano English and the Nature of the Chicano Language Setting." *Hispanic Journal of Behavioral Sciences* 15: 3–35.

———. 2002. *Brown Tide Rising: Metaphors of Latinos in Contemporary American Public Discourse.* Austin: University of Texas Press.

Sawyer, Janet. 1975. "Spanish-English Bilingualism in San Antonio, Texas." In *El Lenguaje de los Chicanos,* eds. Eduardo Hernandez-Chavez, Andrew D. Cohen, and Anthony f. Beltramo, 77–98. Arlington, VA: Center for Applied Linguistics.

Schecter, Sandra, and Robert Bayley. 2002. *Language as Cultural Practice: Mexicanos en el Norte.* Mahwah, NJ: Lawrence Erlbaum Associates.

Silva-Corvalán, Carmen. 1994. *Language Contact and Change: Spanish in Los Angeles.* New York: Oxford University Press.

Silverstein, Michael. 1979. Language Structure and Linguistic Ideology. In *The Elements: A Parasession on Linguistic Units and Levels,* eds. Paul R. Clyne, William F. Hanks, and Carol L. Hofbauer, 193–247. Chicago: Chicago Linguistic Society.

Sommer, Doris. 2003. *Bilingual Games: Some Literary Investigations.* New York: Palgrave.

Suárez-Orozco, Marcelo M., and Mariela M. Páez. 2002. *Latinos: Remaking America.* Berkeley: University of California Press.

Tatum, Charles M. 2001. *Chicano Popular Culture: Que hable el pueblo.* Tucson: University of Arizona Press.

Thompson, Roger. 1975. "Mexican-American English: Social Correlates of Regional Pronunciation." *American Speech* 50: 18–24.

Toribio, Jacqueline. 1999. "Spanglish? Bite Your Tongue! Spanish-English Code-Switching among Latinos." *Reflexiones: New Directions in Mexican American Studies* 2: 115–48.

Torres Cacoullos, Rena, and Fernanda Ferreira. 2000. "Lexical Frequency and Voiced Labiodental-Bilabial Variation in New Mexican Spanish." *Southwest Journal of Linguistics* 19: 1–18.

Urciuoli, Bonnie. 1996. *Exposing Prejudice: Puerto Rican Experiences of Language, Race, and Class.* Boulder, CO: Westview Press.

Valdés, Guadalupe. 1976. "Social Interaction and Code-Switching Patterns: A Case Study of Spanish-English Alternation." In *Bilingualism in the Bicentennial and Beyond,* Gary D. Keller, Richard V. Teschner, and Silvia Viera, 53–85. Tempe, AZ: Bilingual Press/Editorial Bilingüe.

Villa, Raúl Homero. 2000. *Barrio-Logos: Space and Place in Urban Chicano Literature and Culture.* Austin: University of Texas Press.

Villareal, José Antonio. 1959. *Pocho.* New York: Doubleday.

Wald, Benji. 1989. "Implications of Research on Dialects of Mexican American Spanish for Linguistic Theory." In *Research Issues and Problems in United States Spanish,* eds. Jacob L. Ornstein-Galicia, George K. Green, and Dennis J. Bixler-Márquez, 57–74. Brownsville, TX: Pan American University at Brownsville.

Walsh, Catherine. 1991. *Pedagogy and the Struggle for Voice: Issues of Language, Power, and Schooling for Puerto Ricans.* Toronto: OISE Press.

Weinreich, Uriel. 1953. *Languages in Contact: Findings and Problems.* The Hague: Mouton.

Williams, Frederick. 1976. *Explorations of the Language Attitudes of Teachers.* Rowley, MA: Newbury House.

Zentella, Ana Celia. 1997. *Growing Up Bilingual.* Cambridge, MA: Blackwell.

——. 2002. "Latin Languages and Identities." In *Latinos: Remaking America,* eds. Marcelo M. Suárez-Orozco and Mariela M. Páez, 321–38. Berkeley: University of California Press.

——. 2003. " 'José, Can You See?': Latin Responses to Racist Discourse." In *Bilingual Games: Some Literary Investigations,* ed. Doris Sommer, 51–68. New York: Palgrave.

■ INDEX

obligations sets in, 103–6; rules for, 98–100; situational, 100, 103–4; typology of, 101–2

Colorado: language shift in, 51

complementizer *que*, 65

conditional construction, 68

Córdova, New Mexico: code switching in, 105–6

covert prestige, 22

critical linguistics, 6–7

[č] / [š] variation, 70, 82

Detroit, Michigan: language maintenance in, 56

dialect dissing, 12, 14

dialogism, 75

diglossia: bilingualism vs., 42–43

discourse: counter-hegemonic, 71–77; hypothetical, 68; narrative, 66–67

Doran, Amanda, 89–90

Ebonics, 11

education: language of, 48

el don, 75–76

El Paso, Texas: onomastic pronunciations in, 89–90; stylistic discontinuities in, 69–70

embedded language, 95–97

endearments, 37

English: identity and, 15; material prosperity and, 14–15; as official language, 29–30; regional dialects of, 86–89; Spanish-accented, 32; in Spanish discourse, 33–34; in Texas, 87–88

erasure, 17

ethnolinguistic vitality, 44–50; demographic variables and, 46; formal institutional support and, 47–48; immigration patterns and, 46; informal institutional support and, 47;

linguistic status and, 45–46; marriage practice and, 46; social status and, 45; sociohistorical status and, 45; in Tucson, Arizona, 48–49

Ferguson, Charles, 6

Fernández, Rosa, 34

Ferreira, Fernanda, 70–71

Flores, Juan, 13

Floyd, Mary Beth, 51

food names, 88–91

Fortuna, California: language attitudes in, 26–27, 30, 32, 35

fossilizations, 67, 102

Fought, Carmen, 16, 34, 85–86, 87

fractal recursivity, 16–17

free morpheme constraint, 98–100

Fromkin, Victoria, 82

functional domains, 5, 42

Gal, Susan, 16–17, 43

Galindo, Leticia, 82–83, 86

gangs, 34, 85–86

García, Maryellen, 57, 69

Garza, Margarito, 43–44

geography: language attitudes and, 26–28

German-Hungarian bilingualism, 43

Giles, Howard, 44–46

Gonzales, María Dolores, 105–6

González, Norma, 14

government: language of, 48

Gumperz, John, 100

Gutiérrez, Manuel, 68

Haarmann, Harold, 45

Hernández-Chávez, Eduardo, 51, 52

Hidalgo, Margarita, 27–28, 34

Hill, Jane, 11, 12

Hispanic identity: Spanish and, 26–27, 28–29, 30

Holmes, Janet, 22
Houston, Texas: conditional construction in, 68
huachear, 73
Hudson, Alan, 50–51, 52

iconization, 16
identity: code switching and, 34; English and, 15; language attitudes and, 25–30; Mexican American English and, 88–91; Spanish and, 15, 17, 25–30
ideology. *See* language ideology
[i] / [I] variation, 82–83
immigration: ethnolinguistic vitality and, 46; language attitudes and, 26; language shift and, 51–52, 53–58
imperfect tense, 66–67
Indiana: language attitudes in, 28, 29, 35
institutions: ethnolinguistic vitality and, 47–48
Irvine, Judith, 16–17

jainita, 73
Jaramillo, June, 48–49, 70

Katz, Linda Fine, 71–72
Kravitz, Merryl, 33

Landry, Rodrique, 48
language attitudes, 7–8, 20–39; affective dimension of, 21; among bilingual educators, 36; behavioral dimension of, 21, 22; toward code switching, 12, 14, 16, 33–34; cognitive dimension of, 21; communication dimension of, 23–24; definition of, 20, 22; extrinsic orientation of, 23–24; geography and, 26–28; identity and, 25–30; individual nature of, 21; instrumental function of, 22–

24; instrumentalism dimension of, 23–24; integrative function of, 22–24; intrinsic orientation of, 23–24; language ideology vs., 20–21; toward language maintenance, 35–38; toward language variation, 30–35; multifunctional nature of, 22–25; political aspects of, 29–30; sentimental dimension of, 23–24; toward Spanish, 25–30; value/loyalty dimension of, 23–24
language attrition, 41, 64–67
language death, 41–42
language experience, ix; bilingualism and, 3–8; definition of, 7; English and, 79; sociolinguistic discontinuities and, 63
language ideology, ix–x, 3–19; aggregative nature of, 21; bilingualism and, 3–8; definition of, 8; erasure and, 17; flexible nature of, 15–16; fractal recursivity and, 16–17; iconization and, 16; interests and, 9–13; language attitudes vs., 20–21; mediating role of, 16–17; multiplicity of, 13–15; oppositional nature of, 9, 11. *See also* language attitudes
language maintenance, x, 7, 35–38; linguistic capital approach to, 56–58; social networks and, 56; socioeconomic status and, 52. *See also* ethnolinguistic vitality; language shift
language negotiation: code switching and, 104–5
language panic, 10–12, 14–15, 16, 24–25
language pride, 13, 14, 16–17, 24–25, 71–72
language shift, 7, 40–44, 80; definition of, 40–42; immigration and, 51–52, 53–58; in Mexican American com-

munity, 50–52; motivations for, 44–50; recontact and, 55–56; socioeconomic status and, 52; vernacularization and, 84. *See also* language maintenance

language variation, 8–9, 61–63; attitudes toward, 30–35. *See also* language ideology

language wars, 9

la plática de los viejitos de antes, 74–77

Latina gangs, 34

Leone, Elizabeth, 55

lexical gaps, 101–2

linguistic capital, 56–58

linguistic inventiveness, 13

linguistic status: ethnolinguistic vitality and, 45–46

linguistic system, 4–5

locative phrase, 69–70

López Morales, Humberto, 20–21

Los Angeles, California: code switching in, 98–100; language attitudes in, 37; language maintenance in, 55–56, 57; negative concord in, 85–86; phonological variation in, 82; proficiency discontinuities in, 64–65, 66–67; quotative markers in, 87

Luyia, 103

macroacquisition, 84

marriage: ethnolinguistic vitality and, 46

matched-guise test, 30–31, 32, 33

matrix language, 95–97

media: ethnolinguistic vitality and, 47

Mejías, Hugo, 29

Mendoza-Denton, Norma, 34

metaphor, 14

Metcalf, Allan, 79

Mexican: Hispanic vs., 27–28

Mexican American English, 79–93; [č] / [š] variation in, 82; identity and, 88–91; [i] / [I] variation in, 82–83; minority dialect convergence in, 84–86; names in, 88–91; negative concord in, 85–86; phonological features of, 82, 87–88; regional dialect convergence in, 86–89; vernacularization in, 81–84; vowel sounds in, 82–83, 87–88. *See also* code switching

Mexican Americans, x; Hispanic identity among, 26–29; language shift among, 50–52

Mexican American Spanish, 61–77; aspectual distinctions in, 66–67; [b] / [v] variation in, 70–71; complementizer *que* in, 65; conditional construction in, 68; [č] / [š] variation in, 70; locative phrase in, 69–70; proficiency discontinuities in, 64–67; social discontinuities in, 71–76; stylistic discontinuities in, 67–71. *See also* code switching

Mexican immigrant, x

microacquisition, 84

mock Spanish, 12

Muysken, Pieter, 95, 96

Myers-Scotton, Carol, 95, 103

narrative: aspectual distinctions in, 66–67

negative concord, 85–86

network American English, 9

New Mexico: [b] / [v] variation in, 70–71; language attitudes in, 33; language shift in, 51

norms, 22

not exactly, 102

Oakland School District, 11

Ochoa, Gilda, 55

onomastics: pronunciation of, 88–91

Ornstein-Galicia, Jacob, 29
overcoding, 72
overt prestige, 22

para ('to'), 69–70
past tense markers, 66–67
Penfield, Joyce, 29
personal names, 88–91
Phillips, Robert, 70
pinto, 72
place names, 88–91
Pocho.com, 13
Poplack, Shana, 97–98
poverty: language maintenance and, 52, 53
preformulations, 101, 102
prestige, 22
preterite tense, 66–67
proficiency discontinuities, 64–67
Proposition 203, 10–11
Proposition 227, 11

que ('that'), 65
Quebec, Canada: language attitudes in, 45
questionnaires: on language and identity, 25–30
quotative markers, 87

radio announcers, 90–91
Ramírez, Arnulfo, 33–34
rata, 74
recontact, 55–56
refinar, 72
Relampago, 43–44
religion: language of, 48
Rio Grande Valley, Texas: language attitudes in, 29
Rivera-Mills, Susana, 26–27, 29–30, 32, 35
Rodman, Robert, 82

sanamabí, 75
San Antonio, Texas: aspectual variation in, 67; bilingualism in, 79; language attitudes in, 33–34; language maintenance in, 37
Sánchez, Rosaura, 72, 101, 104
San Jose, California: language attitudes in, 33–34
Santa Ana, Otto, 14, 79–80, 82, 88
Sawyer, Janet, 79
Schecter, Sandra, 37, 67
semantic inversion, 13
signage: language of, 48, 49, 73, 107
Silva-Corvalán, Carmen, 37, 64–65, 66–67
Silverstein, Michael, 8
social discontinuities, 71–76
social networks: language maintenance and, 56
social status: ethnolinguistic vitality and, 45
socioeconomic status: language maintenance and, 52
sociolinguistic discontinuities, 63; in proficiency, 64–67; social, 71–76; in style, 67–71
sociolinguistic interview, 83
sociolinguistics, 5–6
Southern American English, 21
Spanglish, 13, 16–17
Spanglish bashing, 12, 14
Spanish: Hispanic identity and, 26–27, 28–29, 30; identity and, 15, 17, 25–30; maintenance of, 35–38; mock, 12; shift away from, 50–52; variation in, 30–35. *See also* Mexican American Spanish
speech community, 62; language acquisition by, 84
standard Mexican Spanish, 33–34
structural linguistics, 4–5

stylistic discontinuities, 67–71
Swahili, 103

■ ABOUT THE AUTHOR

GLENN A. MARTÍNEZ is associate professor of Spanish and linguistics at the University of Texas Pan American. He received a BA in Spanish from the University of Texas Pan American, an MA in Spanish linguistics from the University of Houston, and a Ph.D. in Hispanic linguistics from the University of Massachusetts at Amherst. Martínez has taught a variety of courses in Spanish, applied linguistics, and sociolinguistics at Kenyon College, the University of Texas at Brownsville, and the University of Arizona. He has also served as visiting faculty at the Universidad de Alcalá de Henares, the Universidad Veracruzana, and the Escuela Normal Superior Profesor Moisés Garza Sáenz. He has published more than a dozen articles on issues related to the language of Mexican Americans in the Southwest in journals such as *Hispania, Language Variation and Change, Journal of Sociolinguistics, Southwest Journal of Linguistics, Heritage Language Journal,* and *Critical Inquiry in Language Studies.* His current research interests are in border sociolinguistic theory with particular emphasis on discourse analysis and heritage language pedagogy with a focus on the development of Spanish language literacies.

Mexican Americans and Language is a volume in the series The Mexican American Experience, a cluster of modular texts designed to provide greater flexibility in undergraduate education. Each book deals with a single topic concerning the Mexican American population. Instructors can create a semester-length course from any combination of volumes, or may choose to use one or two volumes to complement other texts.

Additional volumes deal with the following subjects:

Mexican Americans and Health
Adela de la Torre and Antonio Estrada

Chicano Popular Culture
Charles M. Tatum

Mexican Americans and the U.S. Economy
Arturo González

Mexican Americans and the Law
Reynaldo Anaya Valencia, Sonia R. García, Henry Flores, and José Roberto Juárez Jr.

Chicana/o Identity in a Changing U.S. Society
Aída Hurtado and Patricia Gurin

Mexican Americans and the Environment
Devon G. Peña

Mexican Americans and the Politics of Diversity
Lisa Magaña

For more information, please visit
www.uapress.arizona.edu/textbooks/latino.htm